ASSERTIVE DISCIPLINE

Positive Behavior Management for Today's Classroom

by Lee Canter and Marlene Canter

Solution Tree

Design and typesetting by Carolyn Wendt

Cover design by Richard Rossiter

ISBN 1-932127-49-6

Contents

Introduction

When Assertive Discipline was first developed in 1976, the attitude toward behavior management in schools was very different than it is today. Few institutions offered behavior management training as part of their preservice and graduate courses. Few schools included staff development programs that addressed student behavior. Only a handful of books by educational experts were written on the topic. Fortunately, times have changed.

Unlike when we first began training teachers, there is now widespread agreement in the educational community that teachers need to know how to manage student behavior. Increasingly, teacher preparation and graduate education include behavior management as part of their programs. Classroom management is a frequent topic of discussion at educator conferences. Furthermore, national and state teaching standards include requirements for establishing a safe classroom environment that fosters respect and support for all students. Effective behavior management goes hand in hand with master teaching.

The importance of behavior management training has also spread internationally. Over the past few years, we have been invited to speak with teachers in Great Britain, Australia, and New Zealand. Eager to manage their classrooms so that students can learn and they may teach, these educators have embraced the Assertive Discipline techniques and fit them comfortably into their own teaching style and situation.

It is gratifying to know that our program has served education for more than 25 years and has helped more than 1.5 million teachers in the United States and abroad. Assertive Discipline, in various forms, is used in inner cities and rural areas, by teachers of all grade levels and every subject area. Our consultants are asked to provide training for teachers at all levels of experience. The program continues to be valued by new teachers who are struggling through their first year, veteran teachers who are encountering changes in the profession, and administrators who are seeking strategies that work schoolwide.

This increased awareness of the need for behavior management training, plus the positive feedback from educators worldwide, spurred us to write a third edition of *Assertive Discipline*. As you read, you will notice that the basic structure of a discipline plan has not changed. As before, we present skills and strategies for establishing a safe, respectful environment. Teachers, as always, will resourcefully adapt Assertive Discipline to suit their own style and philosophy of teaching.

In this third edition, however, you will find some new concepts and new terminology. Teachers today need to provide feedback to students in a way that is nonjudgmental yet recognizes their efforts and corrects their course of action. Therefore, you will see that we advocate the use of *supportive feedback* and *corrective actions*. This new edition places added emphasis on a proactive approach to behavior management. By assuming that some students will misbehave or test your limits, you can plan how to handle those situations before they have a chance to escalate. Perhaps the most important addition to this new version is the fact that we stress more than ever the value of building positive relationships with students. Trusting and caring relationships with adults is vital for *all* students to succeed—even the most challenging students.

The whole purpose of keeping behavior problems in the classroom to a minimum is to create for students an environment conducive to creativity and achievement. Your students deserve a successful educational experience, with a teacher who cares about each and every one of them. This book will help you and your students reach that goal. We hope that you, like many teachers before you, will read this book, use the plan, and tailor it to your own needs.

MANAGING BEHAVIOR IN TODAY'S CLASSROOM

In order for you to teach and your students to learn, you want to create the optimal classroom environment, one in which your students feel emotionally and physically safe. *Assertive Discipline* offers practical strategies for successful behavior management in a classroom led by a teacher who builds personal, trusting relationships with students. If you are committed to learning these proven techniques, you will have the ability to reach the vast majority of your students.

Chapter 1—Your Role as a Teacher
The first chapter discusses how social developments have redefined the teacher's role.

Chapter 2—A Proactive Approach to Student Behavior
The second chapter examines the benefits of using a proactive approach to help students succeed.

Chapter 3—A Balance Between Structure and Caring
The third chapter offers advice on how to strike a balance between establishing a structured, disciplined classroom while building trusting and caring relationships with students.

Chapter 1

Your Role as a Teacher

You are a teacher. You may be at the beginning of your career, or you may have already collected many years of classroom experience. You may teach in public school or private school. You may teach first grade, middle school, or high school. You may teach math, social studies, or art. No matter what, where, and how long you have been teaching, one thing is for certain: You embarked on your career because you want to help your students realize their potential—academically, personally, and socially.

Above all, you want to make a difference in your students' lives, and as a teacher you are in a unique position to do so. Your students are at school to learn, and you are there to teach them. That's not as easy as it sounds. There are factors that interfere with achieving your goals.

Societal Developments, Changing Roles

Teaching is more challenging today than ever before. Images of a respected authority figure lecturing an attentive group of well-adjusted students reflect a classroom situation of the past. Commanding the attention and cooperation of students simply is not as easy as it once was. The way our society lives and works has changed students and, consequently, your role as a teacher.

As a whole, our society is more graphic and less inhibited than ever before about such issues as sexuality, substance abuse, and violence. In addition, the overwhelmed, often troubled adults in many of our students' lives may not have the time or ability to assist their children to be successful in school and, ultimately, in life. These parents may be dealing with issues such as unemployment, both parents working outside the home, divorce, single parenthood, or poverty. Oftentimes, children must negotiate their way to adulthood without guidance.

Traditionally, the most successful children have had an armor that serves as a strong defense: a supportive home environment. For many of our students, unfortunately, that armor is missing. A lack of parental guidance and involvement leaves many of our students defenseless and alone—unless they meet a caring teacher to fill the gap.

The current conditions in society have brought about a change in your role as a teacher. You can no longer assume that students have been prepared socially or academically at home for the increasing demands of school. You need, therefore, to invest the time and effort to teach your students the behavior and academic skills necessary for success in school.

Lack of Motivation

What happens in school when students do not get the support they need at home? They often do not come to the classroom equipped with an eagerness to learn or with appropriate behavior. As teachers, all of us have worked with students who feel that school is a waste of time and behave accordingly. They frequently are off task, daydream, or engage in disruptive behavior.

These students may not have the self-control necessary to succeed in an environment of high academic and social standards. They are not accustomed to following rules and are more comfortable responding to everyday conflicts with antisocial and aggressive behavior. These are the students who talk when they're supposed to work quietly, who do not complete class work, and who do not turn in their homework. Some students openly defy instructions, and talk back when held accountable. Increasingly, teachers have to deal with students who bully weaker students and who negatively influence others in the classroom.

It's certainly difficult to teach if you need to deal with off-task, disruptive, or angry students. And, correspondingly, it's difficult to learn if off-task, disruptive, or angry students are present in the class.

The Myth of the Good Teacher

Not only do disruptive students interfere with teaching and learning, but they also cause you to question your abilities and effectiveness as a teacher. Oftentimes teachers take behavior problems personally and fall into the trap we call the "myth of the good teacher."

This myth holds that a "good" teacher should be able to handle all behavior problems on her own and within the confines of the classroom. The assumption is, if you are competent, you never need to go to your principal or the child's parents for assistance.

Nonsense. No teacher, no matter how skilled he is or how much experience or training he has, is capable of working successfully with each and every student without support. This myth is especially damaging today because of the increase in the number of students whose behavior is so disruptive that a teacher must have assistance from the principal, the parent(s) and, if possible, a counselor, in order to deal effectively with unacceptable behavior.

The burden of guilt this myth places on a teacher is by no means trivial. According to the myth, if teachers really were competent, they would not have these problems. These guilt-ridden feelings of inadequacy tend to keep teachers from asking for the help they need and deserve.

Good Curriculum Is Not Necessarily Enough

Disruptive students also cause you to question your curriculum and your instructional strategies. Most experts and teachers agree that if the curriculum is first rate, there will be fewer classroom behavior problems. We agree that the better your curriculum and the more varied, motivating, and exciting the instructional strategies are, the fewer behavior problems you will have. In fact, one of the best tools for preventive behavior management is skilled academic teaching.

The problem, however, is that before your lessons ever begin, before you have the opportunity to pique your students' interest with motivating academic material, you must first have their attention. Your students must be seated. They must be quiet. And they must be listening to you.

Good curriculum and motivating instructional techniques will help students stay on task. But first they must know how to *be* on task.

The reality is that you are going to have students who exhibit behavior problems even with the best curriculum and instruction.

Putting aside the current problems in society, the questions you may have about your abilities as a teacher, and your concerns about the strength of your curriculum, let's look at what students need from you and what you can do to influence change.

What Do Today's Students Need?

If you are going to be able to teach, you must have a well-managed classroom. If your students are going to be able to learn, you must help them develop self-management skills that contribute toward their own growth as socially responsible students.

Our goal with Assertive Discipline is to give you a structure for managing your classroom in a way that will allow you to accomplish your academic goals and, at the same time, teach your students self-discipline.

Our experience of more than 25 years training teachers and studying student behavior has revealed some basic principles for effective classroom management. These principles are based on what both teachers and students need in order to enjoy a calm, peaceful classroom environment.

Students need to know your behavioral expectations.

Students cannot be expected to guess how you want them to behave in all situations. If they are to succeed in your classroom, they need to know exactly what you expect of them.

Students need to be taught responsible behavior.

Just telling students how you expect them to behave is not enough. Students need you to take the time and make the effort to teach them responsible behavior. True success and increased self-esteem occur when students first learn how you expect them to behave and then choose that behavior on their own. If students are to be successful in the real world, they must be capable of making independent, responsible choices.

Students need limits.

Students need to know what will occur if they choose not to comply with your expectations. When students are not given the limits they need, they will act up in order to make the adults around them take notice. A student's disruptive behavior is often a plea for someone to care enough to make him stop. In the classroom, that someone is you.

Students need positive recognition and support.

Most importantly, students need to know you will recognize and support positive behavior just as you will limit inappropriate, disruptive behavior. Mutual trust and respect are established when students know they will get honest and consistent feedback from you. In exchange, you will get honest effort from them.

The Assertive Teacher

In summary, a teacher must be willing and able to set consistent, positive behavioral limits while providing warmth and support to students for their appropriate behavior. We call this type of teacher *assertive.*

According to *Webster's New College Dictionary,* the verb *assert* can be defined as: "To state or express positively; to affirm."

We define an assertive teacher as one who clearly and positively communicates her behavioral expectations to her students. The words and actions of an assertive teacher send the following message to students:

"I am committed to being the leader in this classroom, a leader who will establish an environment in which I can teach and my students can learn. To reach this goal, I am committed to teaching my students the behavior they need to allow them to succeed in school. In turn, I will guide them to make choices that lead to success in life.

"I care too much about my students to allow them to behave in a manner that is not in their best interests and in the best interests of the class."

The way to actualize this goal is to develop a proactive approach to behavior management. The subsequent chapters of this book tell you how.

With this commitment and the necessary tools, you can achieve the optimal classroom environment. If you supply the time and the patience, this book supplies the tools. Assertive Discipline will show you ways to teach appropriate behavior and implement a discipline plan that will help students choose responsible behavior, enabling them to learn and to shape productive lives.

REMEMBER...

➤ You chose to become a teacher to help shape students' lives academically, personally, and socially.

➤ Conditions in society and in home environments that lack support leave many of our students with only you to look to as a role model for caring, disciplined, and socially acceptable behavior.

➤ Disruptive students may have caused you to question your abilities as a teacher and the strength of your curriculum.

➤ You can and must teach, encourage, and enforce disciplined behavior to create a classroom environment in which students can learn and teachers can teach.

➤ Assertive Discipline supplies the tools you need to implement a behavior management plan that will help your students choose responsible behavior.

Chapter 2

A Proactive Approach to Student Behavior

The first step toward becoming an assertive, more effective teacher is to reflect on your current approach to behavior management.

As previously stated, some educators believe that management techniques are automatically embedded within instructional techniques. They do not see the need to teach behavior in isolation. The assumption is that students who are involved in relevant, engaging tasks at the correct level of difficulty will not act up. This is true for many students. If you teach using high-involvement techniques, most students will not exhibit problem behaviors. These students will naturally pick up the desired behaviors required for success in each situation.

There are a handful of students, however, who lack self-management skills. They may not have developed the impulse control or attending behaviors needed to work successfully in the myriad activities they encounter in a school day: in cooperative groups, within learning centers, or using manipulatives and doing other hands-on work. They may also be unable to work well in more structured activities, such as whole-group instruction and independent work. While explicit instruction in how to behave is important for *all* students, for *these* students, it will be the key to their success.

What Assertive Discipline research has demonstrated over the last two decades is that in order to establish an effective learning environment, a teacher must teach behavior early in the school year. He must approach the management of behavior with as much thought and planning as he would any instructional or curriculum practice. In short, the most successful way to achieve the optimum environment is for you, the teacher, to use a *proactive* approach. This means that before you meet your students, you will have developed a systematic manner of dealing with behavior, commonly called a discipline plan, and you will have determined all the routines and behavioral procedures you will need for building cooperative and independent behavior. This practice will be beneficial to all students.

Reactive Approaches

In contrast to a proactive approach is one that is *reactive*. A reactive teacher does not have a formal plan for behavior management and would, most likely, deal with misbehavior in a reactive, off-the-cuff manner. Such lack of planning often results in highly charged and emotional responses.

Here is an example of a reactive approach:

When entering the classroom at the beginning of the school day, Pam, a sixth grader with a consistent behavior problem, noisily makes her way to her seat.

Teacher: (*Irritated*) Pam, what's the matter with you? Can't you sit down quietly like everyone else?

Pam: (*Slowly seating herself*) I'm not doing anything, Mrs. Peterson. I'll get to work.

With that comment, Pam turns around and begins talking to the student behind her.

Teacher: Pam, how many times do I have to talk to you? I don't want a day like we had yesterday. Do you understand me?

Pam: What was wrong yesterday? I did my work.

Pam starts to work, but she shortly goes off task and starts talking again.

Teacher: (*Anger rising*) There you go again, young lady. I've had enough. There's no recess for you.

Pam: I'm not doing anything. Jimmy was talking, too, and you didn't do anything to him. You're always picking on me.

Teacher: I'm sick and tired of dealing with you every single day. It's not fair to me, and it's not fair to the other students.

Pam: Well, I don't care about missing recess.

Teacher: What did you say?

Pam: (*Sarcastically, while laughing*) I said, OK, Mrs. Peterson.

Teacher: (*Losing her temper*) That's it. If you don't care about recess, then you're out of here, now. Get to the principal's office.

In this example, the teacher gets carried away with the situation and lets her irritation, annoyance, and frustration with her student's behavior take over. The teacher reacts emotionally to her student's provocation.

Reactive responses are unplanned and counterproductive.

Reactive teachers don't plan in advance how to deal with inappropriate behavior. Rather than realizing the importance of planning ahead, reactive teachers wait until a problem arises and react to it emotionally and ineffectively. Such lack of planning often results in inconsistency. A teacher responding reactively may be rather lenient with one student talking during class in the morning. Yet in the afternoon, because he's tired and more irritated, he may be very harsh with another student for the same offense.

The example above with Pam and Mrs. Peterson illustrates what happens when a teacher does not have a concrete plan for dealing with a student's behavior. Because she didn't address the misbehavior the previous day, the teacher became frustrated by Pam's continued disruption and angrily sent her to the principal. While her removal from the room may have been a temporary reprieve, Pam will certainly be back in the classroom and the problems may continue. The student has missed out on the work, the relationship between teacher and student has deteriorated, and the rest of the class has been taken off task. In such a situation, everyone loses.

Proactive Approaches

Let's go back to the same situation and watch a teacher who proactively plans her responses to classroom disruptions ahead of time so the situation does not escalate.

> *When entering the classroom at the beginning of the school day, Pam, a sixth grader with a consistent behavior problem, is greeted at the door by her teacher.*

Teacher: Pam, that's a really nice outfit you're wearing.

Pam: Uh, really.

Teacher: You look great today. (*Pausing, smiling*) The assignment's on the board. Please sit down and get started on it.

> *Pam goes to her seat and starts on the assignment, but she soon turns around and begins talking to her neighbor. The teacher, expecting possible problems, is nearby and walks over to her.*

Teacher: (*Leaning down, speaking quietly*) Pam, the assignment's on the board. Please remember that the direction for independent work is no talking. Because this is the first time I'm speaking to you, that's a reminder. If you continue talking, you'll have to stay after class for one minute.

Pam: I was just asking what this question meant.

Teacher: I understand. But you need to work on your own. If you have questions, raise your hand and I'll come over.

Pam: I didn't do anything. I am trying to get my work done.

Pam starts to work, but she shortly goes off task and starts talking again.

Teacher: Pam, you've chosen to wait one minute after class. Now pick up your pen and get to work.

Pam slams her workbook shut and crosses her arms in front of her chest.

Teacher: (*Quietly, to Pam*) Pam, come over here with me for a minute. (*To the class*) Class, continue your work.

The teacher takes Pam to the side of the classroom. She positions herself so that Pam's back is to the rest of the class. She speaks calmly and quietly.

Teacher: Pam, I care about you, and I care that you do well in school. That's why I'm concerned about the poor choices you are making in this class.

Pam: What choices? I'm doing everything you're telling me to do.

Teacher: You have a choice right now. You can either go back to your seat to do your work, or we'll call your mom to talk about this problem.

Pam: Really? You're gonna leave class and call my mom right now?

Teacher: No, we'll call your mom together—at lunch. You can explain what the problem is to her.

Pam: I'm not calling anyone.

Teacher: It's your choice to make, Pam.

Pam sulks, turns, and goes back to her seat. Once there, she opens her notebook and gets back to work.

In this example, the teacher planned ahead of time how she was going to deal with Pam. The teacher went out of her way to start the day on a positive note. Before any conflict arose, the teacher was able to show that she cared about Pam as a person above and beyond her behavior in the classroom. Once Pam's misbehavior began, the teacher was able to tap into the positive and caring relationship she had established beforehand to exercise her influence.

Proactive responses are carefully planned and model positive behavior.

Proactive teachers don't wait for poor behavior to occur before developing a plan of action. They determine ahead of time the corrective actions they will use when students are disruptive. They also plan how to positively support students for appropriate behavior. Finally, they teach their students how they expect them to behave. In the example above, the teacher reminded her student of the specific rule she expected her to follow. When the reminder didn't work, she immediately referred to the corrective action, "one minute after class," known to everyone through the discipline plan.

Proactive responses are aimed at stopping the disruption so that the student may get back on task, the teacher may resume teaching, and the class may resume learning. Instead of getting emotionally involved in the situation, the teacher remained focused on the task at hand until the desired effect was achieved: Pam went back to work. Proactive responses are further aimed at giving the student guidance to choose more appropriate behavior in the near as well as distant future.

This book provides the tools you need for developing a more proactive approach toward managing behavior in your classroom. You will learn about developing a plan for correcting inappropriate behavior and for supporting and encouraging appropriate behavior.

All teachers want the best for their students, but that vision is often limited to students' academic success. When you can look beyond their studies and include in your vision the need to teach appropriate behavior, you will have a greater chance of realizing your goals for your students.

REMEMBER...

➤ Reactive responses are counterproductive because they lose sight of the immediate goal of behavior management: to stop undesired behavior and teach appropriate behavior.

➤ Reactive responses preclude the achievement of the long-term goal: to help students move toward self-control and self-management.

➤ Proactive responses are productive because they stop undesired behavior and model socially acceptable behavior.

➤ Proactive responses put the responsibility on the student for choosing appropriate behavior.

➤ Planning is crucial for proactive behavior management. Don't wait until students misbehave before planning how to respond.

Chapter 3

A Balance Between Structure and Caring

At the core of proactive behavior management is a structure called a discipline plan. This plan sets forth the rules and regulations you expect your students to follow. It determines the supportive feedback and the corrective actions you will take should a student not comply. It gives your students clear guidelines for acceptable behavior. It gives you clear guidelines for appropriate and effective responses should emotional or physical conflicts arise.

By themselves, a proactive response style and a discipline plan are not enough to motivate students to change their behavior. If you want students to choose appropriate behavior, they need to know that you are concerned about them—that you care about their personal lives and about their successes in school. Building positive relationships with students and earning their trust sets the stage for motivating them to follow your guidance in the classroom.

If, however, your students do not trust you or do not believe that you genuinely care and want them to succeed, they will not be compelled or motivated to cooperate with you or to comply with your requests. Your behavior management efforts will be doomed to failure. If you do not demonstrate that you care about the student, he will not care about your encouragement or your corrective actions.

Students grow academically, socially, and emotionally in a classroom with a teacher who sets consistent, positive behavioral limits, teaches self-discipline, and at the same time establishes caring relationships that value the uniqueness of each student.

Students grow in a classroom with a teacher who understands that acquiring behavior and social skills is an individual learning process. Such a teacher adapts his teaching plan to allow time for improving social as well as academic performance.

Students grow in a classroom with a teacher who holds all students accountable for both their academic and social conduct. Such a teacher communicates clearly that students have the power to make choices, yet they need to accept the responsibility that goes with it.

In short, students grow in a classroom with an assertive yet caring teacher who knows that she has the power to make a difference in their lives, as follows:

> *"It is the way I perceive the student and the way I act toward him or her that will put me in the position to make some major changes and help the student succeed in school."*

As you implement your discipline plan, you will learn strategies to move beyond the basic plan to a higher form of student self-management. In a safe, peaceful, calm, and predictable classroom environment defined by cooperative, trusting relationships between students and teachers, you will be able to influence your students academically and personally in spite of the problems they may bring to school.

A Continuous, Flexible Program

The challenges in today's classroom are so great that many teachers are on the lookout for *the* teaching method that will spellbind their students and *the* classroom management strategy that will guarantee that their students comply. If you are looking for a quick fix that will solve your students' behavioral problems once and for all, Assertive Discipline is not for you.

There is no quick fix. Motivating students and improving their behavior to help them become responsible individuals takes time and patience. You will undoubtedly want to use the management strategies in this book throughout the school year and adjust them as their effectiveness diminishes.

This is a continual process, similar to the way you employ certain teaching methods all year long to meet specific instructional goals.

As with any framework, you need to adapt Assertive Discipline to your specific classroom. In fact, you may have to adapt the strategies we present in different ways at different times throughout the school year and throughout your career.

For example, you may want to observe the guidelines more closely at the beginning of the school year, since that is a period filled with "first times." Most importantly, it is the first time your students meet you. They need a chance to get to know you and your specific behavioral expectations. That is when you want to follow the strategies for how to create and implement a discipline plan very closely. This means that at the beginning of the school year, you may have to teach your rules and expectations over and over again until they are understood. You may also have to use the techniques to encourage following the rules over and over again until your students have internalized your expectations.

In addition, you may find it useful to follow your discipline plan more closely around difficult periods such as holidays or just before the end of the school year so that your students will not slide back to previous bad habits.

Part of a Larger Picture

While Assertive Discipline suggests the use of corrective actions to help you manage your students' behavior, corrective actions are only part of effective classroom management. In fact, your personal interest in your students' success may be the most important ingredient of your classroom management plan. Effective behavior management is defined by a balance between structure (rules and limits) and a genuine effort to reach out and establish cooperative relationships.

If teacher and student follow the guidelines set forth in this book, the stage is set for a relationship that moves beyond the behavior and recognizes the uniqueness of each child.

REMEMBER...

➤ Following the practical advice in *Assertive Discipline,* you can motivate your students to cooperate by establishing a discipline plan and reaching out to students through proactive relationship building.

➤ Working toward a safe and cooperative classroom is an ongoing process.

➤ Assertive Discipline is not a one-size-fits-all approach. You need to consider your own teaching situation and adapt the strategies accordingly.

➤ Effective behavior management is defined by a balance of structure (rules and limits) and your genuine effort to reach out and establish cooperative relationships.

YOUR CLASSROOM DISCIPLINE PLAN

It's time to move on to developing the practical skills you need for successful behavior management in your classroom. As discussed in Section 1, a structure is needed in every classroom to establish a safe, orderly, and supportive classroom environment in which you can teach and students can learn. A classroom discipline plan will establish this structure. The focus of this section is on understanding and developing your personal classroom discipline plan.

Chapter 4—What Is a Classroom Discipline Plan?
Chapter 4 introduces you to the classroom discipline plan and outlines its components.

Chapter 5—Creating Your Classroom Discipline Plan: Part 1—Rules

Chapter 6—Creating Your Classroom Discipline Plan: Part 2—Supportive Feedback

Chapter 7—Creating Your Classroom Discipline Plan: Part 3—Corrective Actions
Chapters 5, 6, and 7 take you through the steps of developing a discipline plan for your own classroom. The goal is for you to create a plan that is tailor-made for meeting your needs and the needs of your students.

Chapter 8—Teaching Your Classroom Discipline Plan
In Chapter 8, you will find guidelines for developing lessons to teach students your classroom discipline plan.

Chapter 4

What Is a Classroom Discipline Plan?

A discipline plan is the prerequisite for a proactive and well-managed classroom environment that ensures your students' emotional and physical safety and that allows you to focus on teaching, and your students to focus on learning. A classroom discipline plan provides a structure that enables you to clarify the behaviors you expect from students and what they can expect from you in return.

Your classroom discipline plan will allow you to integrate effective behavior management into your teaching routine—whatever your students' grade level and whatever your style of teaching. It is a dynamic, flexible system that recognizes your individual needs as a teacher and the needs of your particular students. Above all, a classroom discipline plan stresses supportive feedback as the most powerful tool at your disposal for encouraging responsible behavior and for raising student self-esteem. It demonstrates your genuine attempt to reach out and build relationships with your students and teaches them that cooperation is in their best interest. Eventually, this process will motivate them to manage their own behavior.

The plan consists of three parts:

➤ **Rules** that students must follow at all times

➤ **Supportive feedback** that students will receive consistently for following the rules

➤ **Corrective actions** that you will use consistently when students choose not to follow the rules

---

Note:

If you have used Assertive Discipline in the past, you will notice new terminology in the classroom discipline plan.

We recommend that you use the terms *supportive feedback* and *verbal recognition* rather than *praise* as part of your plan. Providing feedback to students about their behavior means that you make specific comments about the appropriateness of their behavior, with the intention of keeping them on track. While supportive feedback is positive in nature, it is not evaluative or judgmental like praise can be. The goal of supportive feedback is to help students make good choices for their own sake, not for your approval.

The use of the phrase *corrective actions* is a change in terminology, too. Whereas *consequences* are often associated with punishment, corrective actions mean that teachers are taking actions to help students correct their behavior. Rather than being punitive, the teacher's actions are designed to help the student get back on track and make better choices.

Sample discipline plans are provided on pages 27 and 28. In Chapters 5, 6, and 7 you will look closely at how to choose rules, supportive feedback, and corrective actions for your own classroom.

Sample Discipline Plan for Elementary Students

Classroom Rules

Follow directions.

Keep hands, feet, and objects to yourself.

No teasing or name calling.

Supportive Feedback

Verbal recognition

Individual rewards such as:

>   Positive notes sent home to parents

>   Positive phone calls to parents

>   Positive notes to students

>   Classroom privileges

Classwide rewards

Corrective Actions

First time a student breaks a rule:	Reminder
Second time:	5 minutes away from group, near teacher
Third time:	10 minutes away from group
Fourth time:	Teacher calls parents with student; student completes behavior journal
Fifth time:	Send to principal
Severe clause:	Send to principal

Sample Discipline Plan for Secondary Students

Classroom Rules

Follow directions.

Be in the classroom and seated when the bell rings.

Use appropriate language; no put-downs or teasing.

Supportive Feedback

Verbal recognition

Individual rewards such as:

> Positive notes sent home to parents

> Privilege pass

Classwide rewards

Corrective Actions

First time a student breaks a rule:	Reminder
Second time:	Stay in class 1 minute after the bell, or change seat for remainder of period
Third time:	Stay in class 2 minutes after the bell
Fourth time:	Call parents
Fifth time:	Send to administrator
Severe clause:	Send to administrator

Advantages of Using a Discipline Plan

What will your classroom discipline plan do for you and your students? Following are some of the benefits.

A discipline plan makes managing student behavior more consistent.

Without a clear and preestablished plan for responding to student behavior, you are forced to constantly make choices about how to react to student behavior. As previously discussed, these on-the-spot reactive responses are likely to be arbitrary, inconsistent, and emotional, and thus ineffective and counterproductive. Following the guidelines you establish in your discipline plan will allow you to stay emotionally uninvolved and instead deal with the situation at hand quickly, consistently, and with confidence.

Without a formal plan, teachers often suffer through students' misbehavior until their resistance collapses and they explode in rage.

A plan also provides the basis for teaching self-management. When the system for required school behavior is taught up front to the class, students then have the responsibility to use self-control and make good choices.

A discipline plan protects students' rights.

A discipline plan helps ensure that you deal with each student in a fair and consistent manner. Teachers who do not have a plan tend to react to the students rather than to their specific behavior. Many times a teacher's corrective actions are arbitrary and are based on the history of that student's misbehavior rather than on the situation at hand.

Consider the following:

Early in the day, Kyle talked out in class, disrupting the lesson in progress. His teacher gave him a reminder and continued with her lesson. Later that day, Jamie also talked out, interrupting a student who was presenting an oral report. The teacher, visibly annoyed, disciplined Jamie by taking away her recess. Finally, at the end of the day, when the teacher was tired and her temper a bit frayed, Bradley talked out. This time the teacher lost her temper, yelled at Bradley, and called his parents that night about his problem behavior.

The teacher's irritated reaction to Jamie and her emotional overreaction to Bradley was unfair and inconsistent. And what's more, it most likely created negative tension between the teacher and each student. It will be harder, if not impossible, for them to establish a cooperative relationship in the future.

Every student has the right to be treated fairly and equally. Every student has the right to the same due process in the classroom. Students need to know that when a rule is broken, they will receive a specific corrective action. When your students can rely on fair and equal treatment, they will accept your rules and directions more readily, your disciplinary efforts will be more effective, and the groundwork is laid for you to build positive relationships.

A discipline plan helps increase the likelihood of parental support.

As will be discussed in detail later, you need parental support. You need to know that you can call on parents to support your academic, behavioral, and homework efforts. Before giving that support, however, parents will want to know that you are using a system that is equitable. Parents may become defensive if they feel that the teacher is treating their child differently from the others.

Communicating your classroom discipline plan to parents shows them that you care about teaching their children how to behave responsibly. It also demonstrates your own professionalism and confidence in your ability to manage the classroom.

A discipline plan helps ensure administrator support.

A discipline plan demonstrates to your administrator that you have a well-thought-out blueprint for managing student behavior in your classroom. It shows that you are in control and that whenever there is a problem you will not simply send a student to the office for the administrator to take care of it. When your administrator understands the commitment you have made to effective classroom management, you will be better able to get support when you need it. Ways to ensure administrative support will be discussed in more detail in Chapter 17.

REMEMBER...

➤ A classroom discipline plan consists of three parts:

1. Rules that students must follow at all times

2. Supportive feedback students will consistently receive for following the rules

3. Corrective actions you will use consistently when students choose not to follow the rules

➤ A discipline plan makes managing student behavior more consistent.

➤ A discipline plan protects students' rights.

➤ A discipline plan helps enlist parental support.

➤ A discipline plan helps enlist administrator support.

Chapter 5

Creating Your Classroom Discipline Plan: Part 1—Rules

Each year brings new students to your classroom. They come with their own needs, their own past experiences, and their own expectations. They come with their preconceptions of who you are, what your limits will be, and how they will relate to you and you to them. They want to know: What expectations do you have for us? You need to give them an answer in order to build cooperative and trusting relationships with your students.

Unless *you* know how you want your students to behave, how will *they* know? To successfully manage your classroom, you first have to determine how you want your students to behave. You need to be very clear about what your expectations are and how you will communicate those expectations. As one master teacher said:

"Increasing numbers of students are coming to school from homes where expectations are undefined and rules are either not stated or not enforced. Young people need the structure and guidance that appropriate classroom expectations and rules provide. Today, more than ever, behavioral expectations carry with them an importance beyond the classroom. They help teach what the student may not be getting anywhere else—responsible behavior. When students learn to behave responsibly, their self-esteem rises and their motivation to achieve increases."

As you begin to formulate your classroom rules, ask yourself: *What general behaviors do I need at all times, day in and day out, so that I can teach and my students can learn? What expectations do I have for how students conduct themselves in my classroom?*

How to Develop Rules for the Classroom

Successful teachers have a minimal number of rules that are in effect at all times, in all activities, all day long.

Begin with the basics.

Here are some rules that teachers typically need in order to teach, in order for students to learn, and in order to create a positive classroom environment:

➤ **Follow directions.**
This is perhaps the most important rule you will establish. You can't teach and students won't learn if the many directions you give throughout the day aren't followed.

➤ **Keep hands, feet, and objects to yourself.**
For students to feel safe in your classroom, they need to know that they are protected from being hit or kicked and that their property is protected from being taken or destroyed.

➤ **Use appropriate school language: no put-downs, teasing, or bad language.**
All students have the right to be in a classroom where they will not be verbally or psychologically humiliated.

These basic rules are common to most successful teachers' classrooms. Other appropriate general expectations that teachers have established include:

➤ Be in your seat when the bell rings.

➤ Do not leave the classroom without permission.

➤ No eating in class.

Establish rules that are observable and continually in effect.

What do these basic rules have in common? What makes them appropriate general classroom rules?

First, these rules are observable. They address specific behaviors that teachers can clearly see. The more observable a rule is, the easier it is for students to understand and comply with it. Many discipline plans confuse the difference between goals and rules. It is important to distinguish between these two types of expectations so that you can be fair and consistent, and students can be clear about what to do. Goals are long-range behaviors that comprise the overall climate in the classroom. Examples of goals are: "Be nice" and "Treat each other with respect." Goals are important, but they should not be included in the discipline plan because "nice" and "respect" are open to interpretation and not easily observable. You will want to teach your students behaviors for achieving goals, but as a separate part of your curriculum. Remember, the clearer your expectations, the easier they are for you to enforce, and the easier they are for students to follow.

Second, each of these rules is applicable throughout the entire day. There are no exceptions. The rules apply no matter what activity is taking place. Many times teachers establish general rules for the classroom that are not enforceable throughout the school day or class period. Because these rules really aren't in effect at all times, they can cause more problems than they prevent and actually, through their ambiguity, hinder the teacher's ability to teach students to behave.

Avoid rules that will not be in effect at all times.

With these guidelines in mind, you can understand why you would avoid using rules such as these:

➤ **Raise your hand and wait to be called on before you speak.**
Though this rule sounds sensible, it is not enforceable all day long. There are going to be many times during each school day when students will be expected to speak out without raising their hands first:

for example, in cooperative learning groups, or during transitions. Therefore, this is confusing as a general classroom rule.

> **Stay in your seat unless you have permission to get up.**
Always? Can a student ever get up to get a sheet of paper? To sharpen a pencil? If the rule is not 100 percent enforceable throughout the day, it is not an appropriate general classroom rule.

> **Use a 12-inch voice in the classroom.**
Of course there are many times during the day when you will want your students to speak in a soft voice that can't be heard beyond a foot away. But there are also times when students need to speak up. Again, too many exceptions render this rule unenforceable all day or all period long.

> **Complete all homework assignments.**
This rule sounds acceptable. Obviously, you need students to complete homework. But the problem is that this type of rule does not relate to classroom behavior. There may be times when the student does not understand the assignment. There may be times when completing an assignment is out of the student's control. This rule belongs in a separate homework policy.

Remember, classroom rules must be designed to teach appropriate classroom behavior. When you establish general classroom rules that do not clearly reflect your consistent expectations, you run the risk of confusing students. In truth, you will not be able to enforce these rules with any meaningful consistency. There will always be an element of doubt as to when one of these rules is in force or not. You probably will not be sure, and neither will your students.

Here are some appropriate general classroom rules for different grade levels:

Grades K–3
> Follow directions.

> Keep hands, feet, and objects to yourself.

➤ Do not leave the room without permission.

➤ Use appropriate school language; no teasing or put-downs.

Grades 4–6
➤ Follow directions.

➤ Keep hands, feet, and objects to yourself.

➤ No swearing or teasing.

➤ No yelling or screaming.

Grades 7–12
➤ Follow directions.

➤ Keep hands to yourself.

➤ No swearing, teasing, or put-downs.

➤ Be in your seat when the bell rings.

Each of the rules listed above is observable, and each is a behavioral expectation that can be in effect at all times.

Choose the rules that work for you.

When you develop your own general classroom rules, ask yourself this important question: *Do I want students to comply with this rule at all times?* It is important that the expectations you have for your own classroom fit your needs and the needs of your students. Copying someone else's rules, or ones from this book, will not guarantee that your rules will be effective for you. Use your own judgment and experience to define a set of rules that will ensure everyone's emotional and physical well-being while accommodating your personal teaching style.

Ask students for their suggestions.

Many teachers find it helpful to involve students in choosing some of the rules for the classroom. Ask students these questions: "How do other students stop you from learning?" "What rules would make it easier for you to learn?"

Keep in mind that many times students' rules are more strict than those determined by teachers. Therefore, you should have a clear idea of the rules you would like to include before opening a discussion with your students. As the discussion progresses, guide the students so that their suggested rules are both appropriate and realistic. Consider student input, but be sure that the final rules you choose follow the guidelines in this chapter and your own needs as the teacher.

By including students in your selection of rules, you will give them ownership in the classroom discipline plan. They will see the rules as their rules and will be motivated to support and remind each other about following the rules.

Chapter 6 discusses how supportive feedback will motivate students to follow your rules and choose responsible behavior.

REMEMBER...

➤ Choose classroom rules that tell students clearly what behaviors you expect at all times.

➤ Choose a limited number of rules.

➤ Choose observable rules. Vague expectations are difficult to comply with and difficult to enforce.

➤ Choose rules that apply at all times throughout the day or period.

➤ Choose rules that apply only to behavior. The rules for your classroom discipline plan should not address academic or homework issues.

➤ Consider involving your students in choosing some of the rules for your classroom.

Chapter **6**

Creating Your Classroom Discipline Plan: Part 2—Supportive Feedback

Today you must come to class prepared not only to teach subject matter but to motivate students to behave appropriately as well. It is no longer enough to state your expectations and rules. It is also necessary to motivate your students to comply with them. Without a teacher's committed effort to reach out and keep them on the right track, many students will never build the internal discipline necessary to achieve their potential. While clear, observable rules and expectations provide the foundation for a caring and trusting relationship between students and teacher, motivational techniques will enlist your students' cooperation. One of the most important techniques is supportive feedback.

Supportive feedback is the sincere and meaningful attention you give a student for behaving according to your expectations. Its use motivates students to choose appropriate behavior and creates a positive atmosphere in the classroom that will allow cooperative relationships to flourish. Supportive feedback must become the most active part of your classroom discipline plan.

Benefits of Supportive Feedback

In your classroom, providing supportive feedback will:

➤ Encourage students to continue appropriate behavior.

➤ Increase students' self-esteem.

➤ Dramatically reduce problem behaviors.

➤ Create a positive classroom environment for you and your students.

➤ Help you teach appropriate behavior and establish positive relationships with students.

Let's look more closely at these points.

Supportive feedback encourages students to continue appropriate behavior.

When teachers recognize appropriate behavior, they are providing students with reinforcement for their actions. Thus, the students are more likely to continue behaving appropriately.

Supportive feedback reinforces those students who usually behave by giving them a well-deserved pat on the back. At the same time, it prompts those students with behavior problems to change their behavior. When a student is doing something productive, supportive feedback lets him know and encourages him to keep doing it.

Supportive feedback increases a student's self-esteem.

Supportive feedback can be used to reverse a negative "script" with students who are insecure or used to failure. Your encouragement motivates your students to achieve. The collection of achievements they build contributes to their self-esteem. And when self-esteem is high, effort is increased even more.

Conversely, if the majority of your responses are negative, the self-esteem of your students will suffer. And when self-esteem is low, effort will diminish quickly.

Supportive feedback reduces problem behaviors.

Who receives the most attention in classrooms, the disruptive student or the well-behaved student? We all know it's easy to ignore the "good" child while expending energy on the student who's causing problems. Effective use of supportive feedback turns this situation around.

As a teacher, you know that students are going to vie for your attention one way or another. Assure them that they will receive your attention when they do their work and when they behave appropriately. If you do not acknowledge students for behaving appropriately—if they do not receive the attention they need for behaving appropriately—they will continue to vie for your attention by behaving inappropriately.

By responding positively to appropriate behavior, you quickly teach your students that they can get the attention they want, need, and deserve by behaving according to your expectations. When students learn that you will give them attention for positive behavior, they will choose to act in a positive manner rather than in a negative manner. In turn, they will start to believe in themselves, which is our ultimate goal as teachers.

Consistent supportive feedback helps improve relationships with students.

What teacher would want a school day filled with negativity and tension? Yet that's what many teachers have. If you feel that the only way you can "make students behave" is to reprimand or punish them, chances are your days are filled with tension. You are probably frustrated and so are your students. Overuse of corrective actions will create a classroom environment that pulls teacher and students apart. The overuse of corrective actions and the lack of supportive feedback are major flaws in many classroom management efforts. The more consistently you use supportive feedback to influence students, the better your students will feel about you, the better you will feel about yourself, and the more motivated the class will be to achieve your academic and social goals.

The Trap of Negativity

Now that the benefits of supportive feedback have been addressed, consider these questions: Do you consistently recognize and reinforce students who follow the rules of the classroom? Do you make it a point to always be on the lookout for appropriate behavior? Is "Catch them being good" one of your goals each day?

If you cannot answer with a resounding yes, you are not alone. Classroom observations have consistently shown that approximately 90 percent of teachers' comments to students regarding behavior are negative.

But if supportive feedback is so beneficial, why are teachers so negative?

Why don't most teachers use more supportive feedback? If supportive feedback is so powerful, if hundreds of studies and articles drive this point home, if every book and workshop on the subject of classroom management confirms it, why then do most teachers fail to implement it to its fullest advantage? Why do they, in many cases, forget about supportive feedback completely?

The truth is that, under the stress and strain of the classroom, teachers tend to react negatively to pressure. It is not that they want to be negative. On the contrary, there are sound physiological reasons why teachers respond in a negative manner to negative behavior rather than in a positive manner to positive behavior.

Here is an example of how a person reacts when feeling pressured: First, picture an anxiety-level scale of 0 to 100. At 0 the anxiety level is so low the person is probably asleep. At 100 the person is having a panic attack.

In the classroom, say your anxiety level is at 50 in normal situations. What happens to your anxiety level if a student loudly disrupts the class or refuses to do what you have asked? Your anxiety level will probably rise sharply.

Why would you experience such a dramatic jump in your anxiety level? The biggest underlying fear every educator carries to school each day is that the entire class might get out of control. Simply imagining this can send one's anxiety level skyrocketing. When the anxiety level rises, you respond physiologically. The brain tells you there is a threat and that something must be done immediately. Thus, you might abruptly tell the student to be quiet and provide a disciplinary action in an attempt to quickly lower the anxiety level.

But how do you physiologically respond when students are well behaved? Your anxiety level may drop, but at a very slow rate. There is no voice in your head telling you to do something immediately. No panic. No sense of urgency.

Now, given the natural tendency to react strongly to disruptive behavior, what can you do to circumvent these reactions? How can you keep from falling into the trap of negativity?

Planning to Be Positive

Avoid negativity by planning to be positive each day. To accomplish this, look to your classroom discipline plan.

Every day, your students are expected to follow the rules you established in your classroom discipline plan. When they follow those rules, recognize them for it. As part of your classroom management planning, you should decide ahead of time what kind of supportive feedback you will use. This means developing a variety of ways to reinforce the appropriate behavior of individual students as well as the entire class. The ways you reinforce good behavior are as much an essential part of your classroom discipline plan as are the rules your students are supposed to follow. They are a guideline for your positive reactions, just as the rules are a guideline for your students' behavior.

Reach out and establish positive relationships.

You will have a much greater influence on your students, and they will be much more motivated to follow your rules and regulations, if you have a close and positive relationship. Let them know you care about their life outside your classroom. Let them know you're interested in their home lives, their parents, their siblings, and their friends. Take an interest in their hobbies. Ask them about the things they like and the things they don't. Offer them support with problems in and out of school. Talk to your students. Listen to them. Be there for them. Do so regardless of who they are or how they behave, academically or socially.

This may sound like a lot of work and commitment on your part, but it is not. You will be surprised how much a caring word here and there will accomplish. You talk to your students continually anyway, so you might as well plan the topic of conversation beforehand so that it will serve a purpose.

For example, on Monday morning, ask a student about her weekend soccer game. Recommend your favorite movie to a student who loves movies. Ask a student who enjoys cooking for a favorite recipe. Comment on a new sweater of a student who enjoys fashion. Offer a sympathetic ear to an obviously troubled student—just a minute or two of caring conversation during recess might make all the difference.

Of course, this will not happen by accident. You have to make an effort to reach out to your students. Plan to establish positive contact on personal matters with students as often as possible. A quick exchange about a hobby, a family member, or a weekend activity takes no more than a minute. It is time well spent, considering that your students will feel better about themselves because you made them feel important simply by noticing them for who they are.

Individual Supportive Feedback

Here are some strategies for providing supportive feedback to individual students:

➤ Verbal recognition

➤ Positive notes and phone calls home

➤ Behavior awards

➤ Special privileges

➤ Tangible rewards

We'll take a closer look at each of these.

Verbal recognition is the most powerful positive support you can give.

Your number one choice for positively recognizing student behavior should be verbal recognition. Verbal recognition is the easiest, most meaningful form of supportive feedback you can give. You can give it anytime, in all situations. When you take the time to verbally recognize a student's achievement, you are making a powerful statement. You are saying, "I care about you. I notice the good work you are doing. I'm proud of you, and you need to be proud of yourself, too."

The most important attribute distinguishing successful classroom managers from less effective ones is that they acknowledge their students frequently. These teachers do not acknowledge students by accident. They make a conscious decision: *I will recognize good behavior. I will look for the positive behavior in students, and I will say something about it.*

Send positive notes and place positive phone calls.

Letting your students know that you will send home positive notes to their parents is a great motivator. Just think of its impact. It clearly demonstrates your concern not only about how the student behaves in your classroom, but about your interest in his home life as well.

Just as important as reinforcing students is establishing a positive rapport with their parents. A positive note is one of the most time-effective means of getting parents on your side because it lets them know that you care about their child and want to share in their child's successes. You will need parental support throughout the year, so don't wait until a problem arises to reach out to them. Contact parents early with good news and it will be much easier to get their support when there is a problem.

Here's what a positive note might say:

Sample Positive Note

September 28

Dear Mr. and Mrs. Dawson:

It's a pleasure to let you know what a terrific job Rick is doing in my class. Every day, he arrives in class on time and settles down to work right away. I think you will find that his responsible behavior will be resulting in better grades! You should be very proud of the effort he's making!

Sincerely,

Ms. Lund

Like positive notes, positive phone calls are very effective and don't involve much time or effort—just five minutes a day. Each phone call might take about two minutes. If you place two calls a day, that's 10 a week. In a month, an elementary teacher can make positive contact with each and every parent. At this rate, a secondary teacher can speak to each parent during the semester.

Again, planning is everything. Those five minutes won't just appear in the morning or afternoon unless you schedule them. You have to *make* the time before you can *take* the time. So set it aside—five minutes with a phone. The results are tremendous in terms of increasing a student's self-esteem. When a student feels that his parents and his teacher are working with him, for him, and together, that's motivation.

Here's what a positive phone call to a parent might sound like:

"I want you to know that Sara is really setting a wonderful example for the other students. She follows my directions as soon as I give them, and that helps everybody get to work more easily and quickly. I'm so delighted that she's made such a great start. I feel confident that this is going to be a very good year for Sara. Please tell her that I called and how pleased I am with her behavior in class."

Including parents in their children's successes is a sure way to send positive messages home and bring motivation back to class. Give the added support that will benefit your students. Set a goal to make a specific number of positive parent contacts each week. This effort will greatly enhance your relationship with your students and their parents.

Distribute awards for good behavior.

Special awards for good behavior are a form of supportive feedback that can be motivating for students of any age. Award certificates usually have a long-lasting effect. Students proudly take them home and post them for the rest of the family to see. Parents report that awards often stay on the refrigerator door for months at a time. Keep a supply of behavior awards ready to use and you will see just how effective, motivational, and appreciated they can be.

Here again, plan to send home a specific number of behavior awards each week. In particular, be on the lookout for those students who have to work harder at controlling their behavior, and recognize the extra effort they are making.

See page 50 for examples of behavior awards.

Name

lined up today!

Signed

Date

The Pencil and Paper Award

Presented to

for bringing materials to class!

Signed

Date

Assign special privileges.

Allowing a student to participate in an activity she particularly enjoys is often a great motivator. Verbally recognize the appropriate behavior when awarding the privilege: "You put all the balls away after PE, Amy. That was very thoughtful of you. You can be first in line for lunch."

Here are some suggestions for special privileges:

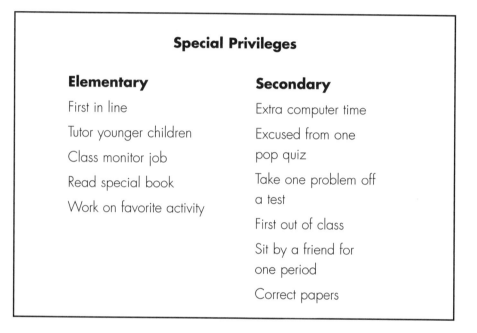

Special Privileges

Elementary	Secondary
First in line	Extra computer time
Tutor younger children	Excused from one pop quiz
Class monitor job	Take one problem off a test
Read special book	First out of class
Work on favorite activity	Sit by a friend for one period
	Correct papers

Offer tangible rewards.

Most of your students will respond to verbal recognition, positive notes, or special privileges. You may, however, encounter several students who will not. A student who comes from a home where supportive feedback is never used may be embarrassed by verbal recognition. Rather than feeling proud, this student may be uncomfortable with your acknowledgment. A tangible reward may hold more interest. It may be the only recognition the student perceives as a positive.

Used properly and with careful planning, tangible rewards are effective motivators for those students who are a bit more difficult to reach. It doesn't matter that the reward is a sticker or a trinket with little monetary value. What is important is that the student earns a reward that can be seen and touched.

Follow these guidelines for using tangible rewards:

➤ Be sure to give the reward immediately after you have observed the desired behavior. You want the student to associate this behavior with the reward.

➤ Whenever you give a student a tangible reward, always pair it with verbal recognition such as, "Rico, here's a sticker for sitting so quietly. I'm really proud of you."

➤ Use tangible rewards sparingly, or they will lose their effectiveness.

Tangible rewards are particularly effective on days when students tend to be overly excited. Fridays and days before holidays or vacations can be particularly trying for even the most skilled teachers. In these situations, you will find that tangible rewards are effective tools for keeping students on task.

Offering tangible rewards is not bribery.

Some educators feel that the use of tangible rewards such as treats, stickers, or small trinkets is bribery. Another way of looking at the issue is to differentiate between the terms, as follows:

➤ A bribe is given in anticipation of a behavior.

➤ A reward is given as a result of a behavior.

➤ A bribe is given to entice someone to do something the person would not normally do because it is not in the person's best interest.

➤ A reward is given in recognition of a behavior that is in a student's best interest.

Finally, bribery is defined as giving an individual something of value to perform an unethical and illegal act. Rewarding students for behaving in a positive manner is neither illegal nor immoral.

There are going to be times when tangible rewards are really the only positives that will work, the only way you can motivate a student. Some students simply need these rewards to get them back on track.

Use tangible rewards, but use them with care.

Classwide Supportive Feedback

Many teachers find it beneficial to plan to recognize and reinforce classwide behavior. These teachers use a classwide supportive feedback system.

A classwide supportive feedback system is a program in which all the students—not just an individual student—work toward a reward that will be given to the entire class. The goal of a classwide recognition system is to have a means to motivate students to learn a new behavior or to work on a problem behavior that the class is having. It shows students how important it is to work together in a cooperative manner to achieve a common goal.

Here's an example of how a classwide system works:

During the first week of school, a seventh grade teacher has decided to use a classwide recognition system to help motivate her students to learn to follow directions quickly and appropriately.

"One of the most important rules you need to learn in my class is to follow directions when I give them. During the past few days we have discussed how you should behave when I give directions for different activities. Now, I have a great idea that will help you get into the habit of quickly following these directions whenever I give them. Here's what we will do:

"Every time I give a direction, I will be looking for those of you who do what I ask. For example, if I say, 'Take out your math books and begin the assignment,' I will be looking for those of you who follow that direction. Then, when I see you following the direction, I'm going to put a point here on the board for the entire class. You have told me that you really want to have free time. So when the class—working together—has earned 50 points, you will earn the right to have 15 minutes of free time on Friday. Any questions?

"Good! Now, please take out your math books. Walter and Juanita have their books out. That's a point for the class. Good work! Eddie and Barbara are ready, too. That's another point."

The teacher marks points on the board as students comply.

Here are four points to keep in mind when considering a classwide recognition system:

1. A classwide recognition system works because it makes use of peer pressure. It's not uncommon for students to cooperatively remind each other, "Hey, listen to the teacher. If we get five more points, we get free time." This is especially true of middle school and secondary students.

2. A classwide recognition system is particularly effective when working on a specific classwide problem behavior. Such a problem might be students noisily entering the classroom after lunch, or students having trouble concentrating on the assigned work during small-group activities.

3. A classwide recognition system is best used during the first month of school to establish "following directions" in a cooperative way. It should be discontinued and brought back only to work on a specific problem or during months such as December and the last month of school.

4. Once your class is running smoothly as a group, you may need to implement an individualized recognition system to help students monitor their "personal best."

Here's how to set up a classwide recognition system:

1. Pick a system you are comfortable with and that is appropriate for the age of your students.

2. Make sure that you are comfortable giving the reward you're offering. Don't choose a reward that you cannot give willingly or one that violates school or district policy such as gum, parties, etc.

3. Be careful that your students are truly interested in the reward. If they are not, the reward will not be a goal they will work toward. If you are unsure, just ask them. Student involvement can help increase interest in achieving the behavioral goals you set.

Here are some ideas for classwide rewards:

Classwide Rewards

Elementary

Game time on Fridays

Special arts and crafts project

Extra PE time

Invite a special visitor to class

Special approved movie with popcorn

Secondary

Radio in class (approved music and volume)

Coupons from student store

Choice of activity

Free reading time

Approved choice of seat for a day

Special celebration treat

Approved movie with popcorn

Note: Save treats and movies for the last month of school, when behavior tends to be more restless. Choose simple privileges for the first month.

4. Make sure your students can earn the reward in an appropriate span of time. Set a goal for how quickly you want the class to earn a reward. Then monitor the frequency with which you are awarding points to ensure that you and the students are on track. Be sure to set reasonable goals. Younger or more immature students should earn a reward in far less time than a secondary class.

```
┌─────────────────────────────────────────────────────────┐
│                                                         │
│            Classwide Reward Time Goals                  │
│                                                         │
│     Grades K–1:      1 day                              │
│                                                         │
│     Grades 2–3:      2 days to 1 week                  │
│                                                         │
│     Grades 4–6:      1 week                             │
│                                                         │
│     Grades 7–12:     1–2 weeks                         │
│                                                         │
└─────────────────────────────────────────────────────────┘
```

5. Once the class has earned points toward a classwide reward, do not take away points for misbehavior. All students, regardless of how many corrective actions they may have received individually, must be allowed to participate in the classwide reward.

Determine a tracking system.

Once you decide to use a classwide recognition system, you will need to have a way of keeping track of the points your students earn. Here are some examples of practical, effective, and motivating programs.

Points on the Board

Designate a corner of your chalkboard to serve as the Classwide Reward Scoreboard. On the scoreboard, write the number of points needed to reach the class reward. Then, when you see a student or a group of students behave appropriately, restate the behavior and put a mark on the board.

> *"Paul, Fusako, and Evan have followed directions and are getting out their science reports. That's a point for the class."*

At the end of the day or class period, total the points. Remind the class of their progress. Each day, at the beginning of class, remind students of the score and the reward they are working toward.

"You have earned 35 points so far this week. Just 15 points more and we will have game time on Friday. Keep up the good work."

Marbles in a Jar

This system is easy to use and is very popular with younger students. The combination of brightly colored marbles and the sound they make as they are dropped into the jar is motivating in itself.

Mark lines on a plastic jar with tape to note daily goals. Place the jar on your desk and tell the students that when they follow your rules, you will drop a marble into the jar. Explain that when the jar is full (or when the marbles reach a certain level), the entire class will earn a reward. Be sure to add marbles throughout the day, otherwise students will lose interest. Remember to restate the behavior you are reinforcing as you put the marble into the jar.

"Leon has his book out already. That's a marble for the class."

Positive Behavior Bulletin Board

This is the most versatile classwide recognition system because you can tailor the theme to the interests of your students. Use your own creativity to create a colorful bulletin board that your students will enjoy.

Your bulletin board should include:

➤ The number of points needed to reach the class reward

➤ A marker indicating number of points earned

Each time you want to recognize good behavior, award a point by moving the marker forward. When the marker reaches the point goal, the class earns the reward. In the example on page 58, the teacher has created a racetrack with 16 spaces. Each time the class demonstrates appropriate behavior, the teacher moves a marker one step closer to the finish line.

Customizing Your Supportive Feedback

Skillful use of supportive feedback means utilizing different approaches for individual students and situations. It means assessing each situation on its own merits and deciding how you, as the teacher, can best meet a student's needs. In every situation, treat your students the way you would want a child of your own to be treated by a teacher.

Supportive feedback techniques are your most powerful behavior management tools. Your knowledge and skill in using these techniques will determine how you view yourself as a professional and whether your students become more successful in school.

REMEMBER...

➤ Use supportive feedback to encourage your students to behave appropriately.

➤ Create a positive classroom environment for you and your students through consistent supportive feedback.

➤ Reach out to students by recognizing their achievements or addressing their concerns outside of your classroom.

➤ Consistent supportive feedback will help you teach appropriate behavior and establish positive relationships with students.

➤ Verbally recognize your students often. It's the most powerful and effective form of supportive feedback you can give.

➤ Set a goal to send home a specific number of positive notes to parents each week.

➤ Set a goal to make a specific number of positive phone calls to parents each week.

➤ Recognize your students' responsible behaviors with rewards.

➤ Motivate your students through special privileges such as extra computer time or being class monitor.

➤ Use a classwide supportive feedback system to motivate all your students to learn a new behavior, or to work on a problem behavior of the entire class.

Chapter 7

Creating Your Classroom Discipline Plan: Part 3— Corrective Actions

Children deserve structure, and they deserve limits. There is perhaps nothing more harmful to children than allowing them to misbehave. Creating a structure within which you set limits is as much a part of a caring relationship as is lending support. You have to show students you care enough about them to say clearly that certain behaviors are not acceptable. What is more, students need to learn that inappropriate behavior carries with it very real consequences. It is true in the real world, and it should be true in the classroom.

As discussed previously, it is your responsibility to let your students know what is acceptable and unacceptable in your classroom. It has been established that your classroom rules will clearly tell students how they are expected to behave in the classroom at all times and that consistent use of supportive feedback will help motivate students to follow those rules. There will be times, however, when students will choose not to follow the rules of the classroom. Whenever disruptive behavior occurs, you must be prepared to deal with it calmly and quickly.

Preparation is the key to managing disruptive behavior. By determining in advance what to do when students misbehave, you will have a course of action to follow that will allow you to stay in control of every situation. By carefully planning effective corrective actions, you will be able to avoid emotional knee-jerk responses that are not effective and, above all, are not in your or your students' best interest.

Corrective actions are not meant to be a form of punishment. They are a technique used to temporarily stop disruptive behavior. They are used to show the student that you care too much to allow continued disruptions. Corrective actions are meant to help the student realize that his behavior does not serve him, and that it is in his best interest to choose more appropriate behavior.

Guidelines for Development

Follow these guidelines when choosing corrective actions for your classroom discipline plan:

➤ Corrective actions must be something that students do not like, but they must never be physically or psychologically harmful.

➤ Corrective actions are fundamental for self-management.

➤ Corrective actions do not have to be severe to be effective.

Take a closer look at each one of these guidelines, noticing how each corrective action is geared to help students choose appropriate behavior.

Corrective actions must not be harmful.

Corrective actions must be something that students do not like, but they must never be physically or psychologically harmful. For a corrective action to be effective, it must be an action that a student does not enjoy: for example, being last in line, getting time-out in the classroom, having to stay one minute after class, missing free time, or having one's parents called. But under no circumstances should a corrective action in any way be physically or psychologically harmful to the student. Corrective actions should never be meant to embarrass or humiliate a student. Above all, corporal punishment must *never* be used with students.

Corrective actions are fundamental for self-management.

Corrective actions are helpful tools in teaching students how to behave in your classroom. Students need to understand that if they *choose* to misbehave, certain actions will occur. When you give students a choice, you place responsibility where it belongs—on the student.

Teacher: Carl, our classroom rule is to keep your hands to yourself. If you poke someone, you will choose to work away from the group. It's your choice.

Carl: OK.

Within a minute, Carl is poking the student next to him.

Teacher: Carl, you poked Fred. You have chosen to sit by yourself at the table.

By helping students see that corrective actions are the result of *their* misbehavior, you no longer become the "bad guy" who gets the student in trouble. The misbehaving student can no longer be seen as the victim of unfair teacher attention: "She's so unfair. Carl didn't do anything. She's just out to get him." The teacher knows, the misbehaving student knows, and all the students in the classroom know: Carl is sitting by himself because of his misbehavior. It was his choice to misbehave. This awareness is a basic step in learning to control one's impulses and managing one's own behavior.

You must be consistent. By assuring that an appropriate corrective action always follows an infraction of a classroom rule, you show students that there is a relationship between how they choose to behave and the outcome of that behavior. This teaches students that they are accountable for their actions. It teaches them that they can make important decisions over their own lives. When you give students choices, they learn that they control what happens to them.

Remember that corrective actions are not punishment. Punishment takes the form of criticism, humiliation, or even physical pain. Teachers who try to curb disruptive behavior with punishment do so at the expense of student self-esteem and growth. Punishment breeds resentment. It does not encourage students to take responsibility for choosing appropriate behavior.

Corrective actions, however, are actions students know will occur should they choose to break the rules of the classroom. Corrective actions must be seen as natural outcomes of inappropriate behavior.

Corrective actions do not have to be severe to be effective.

Many teachers believe that the harsher the corrective action, the more effective it will be in curbing a student's misbehavior. This is not true. For 70 percent of your students, a simple reminder is all it will take to improve their behavior. For another 20 percent, the corrective actions you choose do not have to be severe to be effective. The key to their effectiveness is consistency rather than severity. It is the inevitability of the corrective action that makes it effective. The most effective corrective actions are often the easiest to provide, the most immediate, and the least time consuming to implement.

A fourth grade teacher put it this way:

"Most of the teachers at my school give very severe corrective actions when students misbehave. They have students stay in the classroom at recess or stay after school. The problem is that these corrective actions aren't always convenient for the teacher to implement. Therefore, the teacher is not consistent because it requires too much on his part.

"I found that all I need to do is have students work away from the rest of the class for 5 or 10 minutes each time they misbehave. It's a lot easier on me than keeping students after class. It's a corrective action I can administer immediately, and it works. But it works because I'm consistent about using it."

Here's another example that illustrates this concept. These comments come from a veteran high school teacher:

"After 20 years of working with kids, I've found that the most effective corrective action I can use is to keep a disruptive student one minute after class. One minute after class! That's all. It sounds like nothing, but it works like a charm. In high school, kids can't wait to leave class and be with their friends. That one-minute delay really gets to them, believe me. Everybody's moved on and they're left behind. It wouldn't be any more effective if they had to wait 20 minutes. The beauty of this corrective action is that it's simple for me to use and it's effective."

For 90 percent of your students, all it takes to correct their behavior are verbal reminders and a few simple corrective actions. Probably only 10 percent of your students will cause problems that cannot be corrected that easily. Don't create your corrective actions for the majority of your students with only these 10 percent in mind. Don't fall into the trap of making your corrective actions too severe. Always choose the minimal and most immediate corrective action that will be effective.

Choosing Corrective Actions for Your Discipline Plan

We have looked at what constitutes appropriate corrective actions. Now let's look at how to use them. The best way to organize the corrective actions you choose is to develop a discipline hierarchy as part of your classroom discipline plan.

Establish a discipline hierarchy.

A discipline hierarchy lists corrective actions in the order in which they will be imposed for disruptive behavior within a day. The hierarchy is progressive, starting with a reminder. The corrective actions become gradually more substantial each time a student chooses to disrupt.

When placed in a hierarchy, corrective actions guide students toward self-management. If you begin with a verbal reminder, then move through the hierarchy as disruptions continue, the opportunity is given to the student to control herself before reaching the next step. Since most classroom misbehavior is the result of poor impulse control and bad habits, the hierarchy serves as a verbal and visual guide for students to learn to stop themselves before losing control.

For example:

First Time a Student Disrupts

Most teachers issue a reminder the first time a student disrupts or breaks a classroom rule.

"Alex, the direction was to work without talking. That's a reminder."

"Colleen, the rule in this classroom is no running. That's a reminder."

A reminder gives the student an opportunity to choose more appropriate behavior before a more substantial corrective action is received. It's a powerful reminder, one that carries an important message. The student knows that the next disruption will bring with it a corrective action.

Second or Third Time a Student Disrupts

The second or third time a student disrupts in the same day, the teacher needs to provide a corrective action. Make these corrective actions easy to implement, as immediate as possible, and not time consuming. Typical corrective actions for second or third infractions include changing seats, sitting close to the teacher, being the last to leave, or a one-minute wait after class. If possible, the corrective action should follow the disruption immediately, or it should at least follow within or right after the period during which the disruption occurred.

Fourth Time a Student Disrupts

You need to contact parents if a student disrupts a fourth time in a day. Parent contact is a key component of managing student behavior. For some students, involving parents will be the only way to motivate them to manage their own behavior. Teachers typically give the parent a call or send home a note. There is, however, a very effective alternative method of parent contact. One teacher described how she used it in her class.

"One of my students, Jason, had received his fourth corrective action. In my class that means a call to parents. I told Jason that his parents had to be informed and that he was the one who was going to call them. At recess he completed a behavior journal and we went to the office. I picked up the phone, handed it to him, and told him to call home and explain to his parents that his misbehavior had resulted in their being contacted. When he realized I was serious, his attitude changed. He said, 'Please give me another chance. I'll be good, I promise.'

"I told him, 'Jason, this is the fourth time today I have had to deal with your misbehavior. You are going to call your parents and let them know about it. They need to know that your behavior is preventing me from teaching and you from learning, and that it is affecting other students' ability to learn as well.'

"Well, he made the call, using the behavior journal as a guide. It wasn't easy for him, and his parents weren't pleased. But this corrective action definitely had an effect on him. Since that time, he's been choosing much more appropriate behavior. The very fact that he had to make the call placed responsibility right on his shoulders. It put him squarely in the middle of the situation. I don't think this fact was lost on him."

Regardless of whether the student calls the parent, you call the parent, or you send home a note, the point is that you let the parent know that a student's behavior is disruptive and cannot continue. Students need to know that you will be consistent in the enforcement of this corrective action. And parents need to know where they fit in.

Fifth Time a Student Disrupts

Sending a student to the principal should be the last corrective action in your discipline hierarchy. In preparation for implementing this corrective action, you must have already met with the principal and discussed actions she will take when students are sent to the office (see Chapter 17). You need to know that the administrator will provide the help and support you need. The principal's role might include counseling the student, conferencing with the parents, or even suspending a severely disruptive student.

Severe Clause

In cases of severe misbehavior, such as fighting, vandalism, defying a teacher, or in some way stopping the entire class from functioning, a student would not receive a reminder first. The student loses the right to proceed through the hierarchy of corrective actions immediately. Severe misbehavior calls for an immediate corrective action that removes the student from the classroom.

On your discipline hierarchy, this corrective action is called a *severe clause*. Here's an example of how to implement the severe clause:

> *A student becomes angry with a classmate and begins loudly yelling and punching him. The teacher walks up to the student and calmly states, "There is no fighting allowed in this classroom. You know the rule. You have chosen to go to the principal's office immediately. We will discuss this later."*

Why is a severe clause necessary? If a student severely disrupts the classroom, that action is stopping the education process. You are unable to teach and other students are unable to learn. Removing the student returns control of the classroom to you and provides the disruptive student a chance to calm down before corrective measures are introduced. Removing the student shows that you will not tolerate behavior that endangers the physical or emotional safety of your students or yourself. A severe clause addresses the severity of a student's actions. It sends a message that certain behaviors are simply beyond limits.

Sample Discipline Hierarchies

Here are some sample discipline hierarchies that adhere to the guidelines above:

Sample Discipline Hierarchy for Grades K–3

First time a student breaks a rule:	Reminder
Second time:	5 minutes working away from the group (near teacher)
Third time:	10 minutes working away from the group
Fourth time:	Call parents
Fifth time:	Send to principal
Severe clause:	Send to principal

Sample Discipline Hierarchy for Grades 4–6

First time a student breaks a rule:	Reminder
Second time:	10 minutes working away from the group (near teacher)
Third time:	15 minutes working away from the group, plus write in behavior journal
Fourth time:	Call parents
Fifth time:	Send to principal
Severe clause:	Send to principal

Sample Discipline Hierarchy for Grades 7–12

First time a student breaks a rule:	Reminder
Second time:	Stay in class 1 minute after the bell
Third time:	Stay in class 2 minutes after the bell, plus write in behavior journal
Fourth time:	Call parents
Fifth time:	Send to principal or administrator
Severe clause:	Send to principal or administrator

You can see from these sample hierarchies that the corrective actions become more substantial each time a rule is broken. They follow a natural order that students will learn to expect.

A discipline hierarchy outlines your expectations for behavior.

The value of a discipline hierarchy as part of your classroom discipline plan is that everyone—students, parents, administrators, and, most importantly, you—knows exactly what is going to happen each time a rule is broken.

You won't react emotionally and erratically, because you won't have to stop what you're doing to figure out what to do next. The hierarchy is a tool for you to remain calm and in control no matter how many students disrupt in a given day.

Likewise, students will know exactly what they can expect each time they break a rule. The hierarchy becomes a tool for the student to learn self-control.

The proactive steps you take when planning your corrective actions increase your effectiveness as a classroom manager. These steps assure that your responses will be consistent and fair no matter if you are tired, distracted, or in a good or bad mood.

Keeping Track of Corrective Actions

For your discipline hierarchy to work, you will need a system to keep track of student misbehavior and corrective actions accrued. You will need to know at a glance the names of students who have received corrective actions and where the students are on the hierarchy. Record the reminder, as well as every other corrective action the student has received.

More work for you? It doesn't have to be.

Your record keeping should be practical and simple.

Some teachers use a clipboard to record students' names and the number of times they have broken a rule. Others record this information in their plan book or in a classroom management logbook. Whatever system you use, it must be easily accessible to you as you teach. The easier it is, the less additional work it will be for you.

Here is an example of how effective record keeping can work:

During class JoAnn is bothering another student. Her teacher calmly says to her, "JoAnn, the rule is 'Keep your hands and feet to yourself.' This is a reminder." The teacher then writes JoAnn's name on her clipboard.

Later the same day, JoAnn begins talking loudly during quiet reading time. The teacher quietly reminds JoAnn, "This is the second time you have misbehaved. You have chosen to sit by yourself in the back of the room." The teacher then places a check next to JoAnn's name on the clipboard to indicate that she has received the second corrective action.

At the end of the day, the teacher removes the sheet from the clipboard and places it in a permanent three-ring binder, or transfers the information to her record book. The teacher then has permanent documentation of the student's misbehavior and how it was handled.

Note:

In the first edition of *Assertive Discipline*, names and checks on the chalkboard were thought to be essential to the program, but they are not. This particular practice was first suggested after having watched teachers interrupt their lessons to make negative comments to misbehaving students. Writing the student's name on the board was intended to warn the student in a calm, nondegrading manner. It would also provide a record-keeping system for the teacher.

Unfortunately, some individuals have misinterpreted the use of names and checks on the board as a way of humiliating students. Instead, teachers should write the disruptive student's name on a clipboard or in a record book and calmly say, for example, "David, you talked out. That's a reminder."

Behavior documentation is also meant to help you keep track of your students' progress throughout the school year. You will soon notice that using the effective classroom management tools presented in *Assertive Discipline* helps your students choose appropriate behavior in line with your behavioral expectations. You will see that most of your students don't have a behavioral problem, but that their misbehavior is motivated by the natural and desired exuberance of youth. You will notice that most of your students' behavior can be improved easily. In fact, you will realize that you don't have as many difficult students as you thought. Your attitude toward your students will improve, and your anxiety level when entering the classroom will diminish.

Each student must start each day with a clean slate.

The corrective actions a student accumulates during one day should never roll over to the next day. You never want a student to think, *Well, I've already got two strikes against me from yesterday, so why should I behave today?* You and your students need to begin each day with the highest of expectations. Keep sight of the fact that your goal is positive: You want your students to learn to manage their own behavior.

Suggested Corrective Actions for Your Classroom

There are many possible corrective actions to use in your classroom. Whichever ones you choose, make sure they will work for you and your students.

➤ Corrective actions must be appropriate for your students, and you must feel comfortable using them.

➤ Choose corrective actions that are easy for you to implement.

➤ Choose corrective actions that your students will respond to.

➤ Don't choose corrective actions just because they have been suggested in a book or because they work for other teachers. If a corrective action is difficult for you to use, you will be less inclined to actually do so. Consistency is the key to the success of your discipline plan. Be realistic about your own teaching style. Know what you really are willing and able to do consistently.

Time-Tested Ideas You May Want to Use

Teachers have found the following corrective actions to be effective in the discipline hierarchy, particularly the second or third time a student breaks a rule.

Time Out—Removing a Student from the Group

Removing a disruptive student from the group is not a new concept, but it is a very effective corrective action for elementary-age students. Designate a chair or table at the side of the room as the time-out area. Depending on the age of the student, a trip to the time-out area could last from 5 to 10 minutes. (Note: It's important that students not be isolated from the rest of the class for long periods of time. Keep your time within the limits.) While separated from the rest of the class, the student continues to do his work.

Use a timer. It's hard to keep track of the minutes when you're busy teaching class. Put the timer by the time-out area. When the student goes to the area, he turns the timer to the correct number of minutes. When the timer goes off, the student rejoins the class.

Using time-outs may not be effective or desirable with difficult students. In part, a difficult student's misbehavior is *meant* to set him apart from a group. Having a difficult student work away from the group may isolate him even more. A difficult student may benefit more from working in close proximity to the teacher rather than in a time-out area. If you are close to a difficult student, it will be easier for you to monitor his behavior and, if necessary, correct it immediately without having to interrupt the flow of the class. (Refer to Section 4 for individualized discipline plans more appropriate for students with a serious behavior problem.)

One-Minute Wait After Class

It sounds deceptively simple, but this is a corrective action that students do not like. Therefore it works. You simply have the student wait one minute after the other students have been dismissed for recess, lunch, home, or the next period. One minute may not seem like a lot of time to you, but it can be an eternity to a student who wants to be first in line at handball, for lunch, or on the bus, or who wants to walk to the next class with friends. Don't underestimate the power of this corrective action. Secondary teachers in particular find it surprisingly effective.

During the one-minute wait, you can take the opportunity to briefly counsel the student regarding her disruptive behavior. This corrective action can be effective for all age levels.

Written Assignment in Behavior Journal

You want more from corrective actions than a student's feeling of contrition about what he did. You also want the student to learn from the experience. You want him to think about his behavior and how he can choose to behave differently in the future.

When a student breaks a classroom rule, have her write an account of the misbehavior during recess, after class, or at home. The account should include the following points:

1. Why the student chose to break the rule or not follow the direction

2. What alternative action the student could have taken that would have been more appropriate

The student should sign and date the account. The report should then be added to the student's documentation records. (A copy can also be sent home to parents as documentation of a student's misbehavior.)

This activity helps students accept responsibility for their behavior and think about choosing alternative behaviors in the future. This is an appropriate activity for upper-elementary through middle-secondary students.

The behavior journal is the foundation of one ninth grade science teacher's disciplinary corrective actions. Here is her rationale for using the journal:

> *"I find there are so many students today who have not been taught to take responsibility for their behavior. It's our job as educators to teach them to take responsibility for their actions, to help them recognize the consequences their actions bring, and to focus on teaching them alternative behaviors.*

"When a student is disruptive in my class, I ask the student to write in the journal. I then use the journal as the focus of a meeting with the student to discuss how we can work together to improve his behavior. These meetings are usually brief, to the point, and highly effective. The student learns that I care and that I expect him to take responsibility for his behavior.

"If the meeting does not solve the problem, however, I'm prepared to take the next step. I ask the student to take the journal home to discuss with his parents. A parent is to sign the journal, and the student brings it back to school.

"Sending the journal home serves two purposes. First, the student does not enjoy showing it to parents or having to discuss his behavior. So it serves as a deterrent. Second, the journal clearly documents to parents how their child is behaving. When and if I need to make a call to these parents, I know that they're already aware of a problem and that there will be much more support waiting."

Note:

Misbehavior that occurs outside the classroom in common areas of the school must be addressed by a separate schoolwide discipline plan. A schoolwide discipline plan carries with it a separate set of corrective actions that students receive at the time of an infraction and does not impact your classroom discipline plan.

REMEMBER...

➤ If disruptive behavior occurs, you must deal with it calmly, quickly, and consistently.

➤ Be prepared. Decide on corrective actions that students receive should they choose to disregard the rules of the classroom.

➤ Corrective actions

1. are fundamental to self-management.

2. do not work in isolation. They must be balanced with positive support.

3. do not have to be severe to be effective.

4. must be appropriate for your students, and you must be comfortable using them.

5. must be ones that students do not like, but they must never be physically or psychologically harmful.

6. should be organized into a hierarchy that clearly spells out what will happen from the first time a student breaks a rule to the fifth time the same student breaks a rule the same day.

➤ The first corrective action should be a reminder.

➤ Parent and administrator contact should appear near the end of the hierarchy.

➤ The hierarchy should include a severe clause for dealing immediately with severe misbehavior.

Chapter 8

Teaching Your Classroom Discipline Plan

Once you have decided on your general classroom rules, the supportive feedback you will give when rules are followed, and the corrective actions you will take when your students choose to break the rules, your classroom discipline plan is complete.

Now, in order to make the plan work effectively in your classroom, you must teach it to your students. This is critical. Don't just write your plan on a poster or read it out loud to students. Teach your plan.

If you want students to learn an academic subject, you have to teach them. If you want students to behave, you have to teach them that, too. View the teaching of behavior in the same light as you view the teaching of academics. Teaching your discipline plan to your students is as important as any lesson you will teach during the year. This lesson should take place the first day of school (or, if you are introducing the discipline plan in the middle of the year, as soon as you have completed your plan).

Reteach your discipline plan, or portions thereof, every time more than just a few students repeatedly misbehave and your classroom seems to get out of order. This may be a sign that your students have "forgotten" all or just some elements of your discipline plan. Refreshing their memories will be more effective than issuing one corrective action after another to reestablish order in your classroom. After all, if your students have forgotten a math, science, or language lesson, you would reteach it.

As with any academic lesson, make sure you use teaching techniques and teaching aids that work for you. Practice what you want to say and how you want to say it. Make your performance count: use visual aids where appropriate, and role-play—use your imagination to make your lesson on behavior as engaging as any other lesson you teach.

Follow the guidelines presented in the sample lessons that follow. There is sample dialogue, but you should gear your lesson to fit the needs and age of your own students. As you read, keep this thought in mind: All students, no matter what their age, need a clear explanation of your rules, corrective actions, and supportive feedback at the start of the school year or at the introduction of the plan.

Each lesson covers the following sequence:

1. Explain why you need rules.

2. Teach the rules.

3. Check for understanding.

4. Explain the supportive feedback you will use when students follow the rules.

5. Explain why you have corrective actions.

6. Explain the corrective actions.

7. Check for understanding.

Grades K–3: Teaching Your Classroom Discipline Plan

With students in grades K–3, you will want to spend plenty of time teaching your lesson, making sure that all of them understand the importance of each of your rules and how they are to follow them. Examples, discussion, and role-play will enhance student participation and understanding. Likewise, the role that supportive feedback and corrective actions play in your plan must be made clear to your young students.

1. **Explain why you need rules.**

   Teacher: How many of you have rules at home? *(Wait while students raise hands.)* Jennifer, what's a rule that you have in your home?

   Jennifer: Play in the yard, not in the street.

   Teacher: That's a really smart rule. Why do you think your mom wants you to follow this rule?

   Jennifer: So I won't get hurt.

   Teacher: That's right. She wants you to be safe, so she has rules that will help keep you safe. OK, who else wants to share a rule you have at home?

   Continue sharing rules from home. Talk about why these rules are important to the safety and well-being of the students. Tell students that just as it's important to have rules at home, it's also important to have rules at school.

   Teacher: You have rules at home to keep you safe. We also have rules here at school that help make it a place where we all can learn. Who can tell me some of the things that might happen at school if we didn't have any rules at all? *(Share responses.)*

2. **Teach the rules.**

   Teacher: In our class, we're going to have three very important classroom rules that I expect you to follow all the time. One of the rules of our classroom will be "Walk, don't run, in the classroom." This is a very important rule for all of us. When you're at home, do you ever run through the hall, or into the kitchen, or in your room? I'm sure you do! Now look around you. Why do you think it would not be a good idea to run here at school?

Jasmine: Because there are so many students here, and you could bump into them.

Teacher: That's right! Someone could trip. Someone might fall. Someone could get hurt. And it could get very noisy. That's why we need the rule "Walk, don't run, in the classroom."

Role-play the rule. Give students the opportunity to demonstrate following this rule.

Teacher: OK, let's practice following this rule. Nadia, would you please return this book to the reading corner following the rule "Walk, don't run, in the classroom"? (*Nadia picks up the book and walks back to the reading corner.*) That's excellent! Thank you, Nadia. That's exactly how we all need to walk when we're in the classroom. Quietly and slowly, so none of us is disturbed or bumped into.

Continue teaching all your rules in this manner.

3. **Check for understanding.**

Take the time to make sure all students understand the rules you have taught them.

Teacher: Who can tell me again what our first classroom rule is? (*Stacy answers.*) Thumbs up, class, if you agree with Stacy. That looks like everyone!

Teacher: Kiana, when is it OK to run in the classroom?

Kiana: Never!

Teacher: Keith, if you need to get a sheet of paper in a big hurry, should you ever run to the paper box?

Keith: No!

Teacher: Can you explain why not?

Keith: We don't want to bump into or hurt someone.

Teacher: That's right. We're going to practice this on the way to the art room. When I say, "Line up," I want you to stand up and walk to the door. I want to see everyone following the classroom rule "Walk, don't run, in the classroom."

Ready? Line up at the door. (*Class lines up.*) Jeff is walking. So are Carla and Cecilia. Everyone is following the rule! Terrific!

4. **Explain the supportive feedback you will use when students follow the rules.**

Supportive feedback is the most important part of any behavior management plan. This is the time to let your students know how much value you place on recognizing their good behavior.

Teacher: We have just been discussing our classroom rules. Now I want to tell you what will happen when you follow them. You will notice that I'm really going to pay attention to good behavior. When I see you following the rules, I will let you know that you are following the rules correctly. I will also be sending home notes to your parents, telling them how terrific you have been. Sometimes I will even give them a phone call! I will be giving special awards to you, too. In my class, good behavior will get attention!

5. **Explain why you have corrective actions.**

Miguel: Well, what will happen when we don't follow the rules?

Teacher: That's a fair question. After all, none of us is perfect. We all have trouble at times following rules. Let's talk about this for a moment. Miguel, what might happen at home if you broke an important rule?

Miguel: I can't watch TV or play with my friends.

Teacher: Miguel, you know that your parents aren't doing this to be mean. They want you to learn to behave in a safer way. At school, I want to help you learn to behave in a safe way also. When you break a classroom rule, you need to learn that something will happen. Something you probably won't like very much.

6. **Explain the corrective actions.**

Teacher: I'm going to keep this clipboard near me during the day. (*Hold up clipboard.*) The first time you break a rule and disrupt the class, I will write down your name. I will also remind you of what the rules are. For example, if you are running in the classroom, all I will say to you is, "John, the rule is no running in the classroom. That is a reminder." If you are teasing your neighbor, I will say, "Mia, the rule is no teasing. That's a reminder." That's all that I will do. This reminder gives you a chance to choose better behavior. And I know that you will choose better behavior.

But if you do break this rule again or any other rule during the day, I will put a check next to your name. (*Show check next to name on clipboard.*) This means that you have broken a rule two times. And this means that you have chosen to sit for five minutes away from the group. This will give you time to calm down and think about your behavior.

Go through the rest of the discipline hierarchy in this manner, explaining each corrective action. Afterward, take the time to emphasize your belief that the students can behave and act responsibly.

Teacher: I know you can follow our classroom rules. I know that all of you can make good decisions about how to act in class. I hope that none of you chooses to go to time-out, or have me call your parents, or go to the principal.

7. **Check for understanding.**

Teacher: Who can tell me the first thing I will do when a rule is broken?

Ling: We get a reminder.

Teacher: That's right, Ling. I will give a reminder. The helpful thing about a reminder is that it gives you a chance to stop, think about your behavior, and make a better choice. Now, what happens the second time a rule is broken?

Make sure that all students understand what will happen each time a rule is broken. With young students, you will have to review the corrective actions frequently.

Grades 4–6: Teaching Your Classroom Discipline Plan

Students in grades 4–6 want to understand the reasons behind your classroom rules. Explain why they need rules. Tell them how your rules will help them do better in school. Relate how rules will affect them in other areas of their lives.

1. **Explain why you need rules.**

Teacher: I want to make sure this is a great year for all of you. I also want to make sure all of you are able to learn as much as you possibly can. To make certain this happens, we need to talk about how I expect you to behave in this classroom.

This is important because in this classroom you have the right to learn in a safe and pleasant environment. To make sure that all students can enjoy this right, you have the responsibility of following our classroom rules.

Talk about other rules students have in their lives. Ask students to share some of the rules they have at home.

Teacher: What are some of the rules that you have outside of school? *(Talk about rules that students have experienced outside of school: for example, rules at home, traffic rules, safety rules at theaters, camp, or after-school programs.)* Why do we have these rules? Why are these rules enforced? *(Tell students that just as it's important to have rules at home or to have traffic rules, it's also important to have rules at school.)*

Why do you think we have to have rules at school? *(Share comments.)* Having rules will help make it a safe place to learn. Also, when we have rules, you will know exactly how I expect you to behave. You will never have to say, "I didn't know we weren't supposed to . . ."

2. **Teach the rules.**

Teacher: The first rule we have in our classroom is "Follow directions." During the day, I will be asking you to do lots of different things. I will be giving you many, many directions. Can anyone give me some ideas of what those things might be? *(Share responses: for example, pass your papers forward, clear your desks, go to your reading groups, take your books out.)* That's right! Why do you think it's important that you follow my directions when I give them?

Sam: If we don't, we might waste time.

Teacher: You're right, Sam. We have so much to do each day,
           and I want to be sure we get it all done. Another rea-
           son to follow directions is that it helps us to be safe. If
           I dismiss you for recess and everyone races for the
           door, someone might get hurt.

3. **Check for understanding.**

Teacher: Now let's take a minute to review what a direction is.
           How can you be sure when I am giving you a direc-
           tion? Kenny, what's a direction?

Kenny: When you tell us to do something.

Teacher: That's right. A direction is any time I ask you to do some-
           thing. Now, please clear your desks. Put everything away.
           (*Pause. Look around the room.*) I see that you listened. You
           followed the direction. And now we're all ready to do
           whatever's coming up next! See how well we can get
           things done? I know all of you can follow this rule.

*Continue in this manner teaching each of your classroom rules. To help
students remember the rules, place a chart on the wall or write the rules
on the board.*

4. **Explain the supportive feedback you will use when students follow the rules.**

*Supportive feedback is the most important part of any behavior man-
agement plan. Now's the time to let your students know how much value
you place on recognizing their good behavior. The supportive feedback
you give will encourage them to repeat the behavior.*

Teacher: We have just been discussing our classroom rules.
           Now I want to tell you what will happen when you

follow them. You will notice that I'm really going to pay attention to good behavior. When I see you following the rules, I will let you know what a great job you're doing. I will be sending home notes to your parents, telling them how terrific you have been. Sometimes I will even give them a phone call! I will be giving good behavior awards to you, too. In my class, good behavior will get attention!

5. **Explain why you have corrective actions.**

Teacher: You're probably wondering what will happen when you break one of our classroom rules. This is what will happen: When you choose to break a rule, and it is your choice, you will receive a corrective action. *(Pause.)* This will help you think about the choices you make. You all are becoming responsible young people, and I want to help you make good choices. You need to understand that when you don't make good choices, certain actions will occur.

In this class, I have what I call a discipline hierarchy. This hierarchy lets all of us know what will happen if you disrupt one time during the day and what will happen the second time, third time, fourth time, and fifth time you disrupt. This is my discipline hierarchy. *(Put up a poster listing all corrective actions, or write them on the board. The hierarchy should be left up for students to become familiar with.)*

6. **Explain the corrective actions.**

Teacher: Please read the hierarchy to yourself. We will discuss it when you're done. *(Allow a few minutes for your students to read through the hierarchy of corrective actions.)* OK, those are the corrective actions.

The first time you choose not to follow a rule, I will write your name on the clipboard. (*Hold up clipboard.*) I will also remind you what the rules are. For example, if you are talking when you should be doing independent seat work, all I will say to you is, "John, the rule is no talking during seat work. That is a reminder." That's all I will do. If you have trouble following this rule or another rule during the day, I will put a check next to your name. This means that you have chosen to receive a corrective action. As you can see on the discipline plan, that corrective action is to sit for five minutes away from the group. This will give you time to calm down and think about your behavior.

Go through the rest of the disciplinary hierarchy in this manner, explaining each corrective action. Afterward, emphasize your belief that the students can behave and act responsibly.

I believe that all of you can follow our classroom rules. I have confidence that all of you can make good decisions to choose behavior that makes our classroom a place where we all can learn and get along together. I hope that none of you will choose to remain after class, have me call your parents, or go to the principal.

7. Check for understanding.

Question students to make sure they understand the corrective actions and how the hierarchy works. Make sure that students understand that these corrective actions will be given every time they choose to misbehave. Students must learn that the corrective actions are inevitable. With this knowledge, they will learn that they are accountable for their actions and have control over the corrective actions by the way they choose to behave.

Grades 7–12: Teaching Your Classroom Discipline Plan

For students in grades 7–12, teach your rules in a more matter-of-fact manner. These students have been exposed to classroom rules before, so you can be brief and to the point. Give a brief rationale for each rule and state your expectation that all students will follow the rules. To make your lesson as meaningful as possible, relate the rules to the real world that they will soon be entering.

Keep in mind that secondary teachers often make the erroneous assumption that students should just know how to behave. Remember that your classroom is unique, and you have your own unique set of expectations that need to be communicated.

1. **Explain why you need rules.**

   Teacher: In this classroom, I have three rules that will be in effect at all times. I will explain the rules in just a moment. First, though, I want all of you to clearly understand why I have rules.

   It's simple. I need to be able to teach, and you need to be able to learn. For both of those actions to happen, we all need appropriate behavior in the classroom. I know you're familiar with following rules. You have to follow traffic rules if you want to drive. You have to follow your boss's rules when you're at work. These rules are in place for safety reasons and to help get a job done. It's no different in this classroom. I have rules so we can get our job done here. And just as you have to follow traffic rules and rules on the job, I expect you to follow the rules in my classroom.

2. **Teach the rules.**

   Teacher: My first rule is "Follow directions." This means that when I give any direction to you, such as open your books, take out your notebooks, or pass your papers forward, I expect you to follow the direction immediately. We have lots to do in this class, and I don't want to waste any of your time or mine asking over and over again for something to be done. When I give a direction, I expect you to follow it.

Continue explaining each of the rules.

3. **Check for understanding.**

Teacher: Does anyone have any questions about these rules?

4. **Explain the supportive feedback you will use when students follow the rules.**

Teacher: Now that we have talked about the classroom rules, let's talk about what happens when you follow these rules. I'm a lot more interested in recognizing you for appropriate behavior than I am in pointing out inappropriate behavior. You will notice this year that I will be on the lookout for students who follow the rules, and I will let you know that your efforts are noticed.

Throughout the year, I will be passing out coupons for the student store, sending notes home to parents, and letting you know in other ways that I recognize the fact that you're choosing to follow the rules of this classroom. I just think it makes sense to let you know that you're doing a good job. We all like a pat on the back once in a while, and I plan to be giving a lot of those this year!

5. **Explain why you have corrective actions.**

Teacher: I expect all of you to follow the rules of the classroom. But to be realistic, it may not always work out that way. You are young adults now, and you are responsible for your behavior. When you make poor choices in what you do, oftentimes there are corrective actions. It's true in the workplace, it's true at home, and it's true here at school.

6. **Explain the corrective actions.**

Teacher: In this classroom, I have what I call a discipline hierarchy. You can see it posted on the wall in front of the room. *(Point to hierarchy.)* Please take a few minutes to read it. *(Pause for reading.)* As you can see, the hierarchy clearly spells out what will happen the first time a rule is broken, and the second time, third time, fourth time, and fifth time. Let's go through it. What happens the first time you choose to disrupt?

Alicia: You will write my name down and I will be given a reminder.

Teacher: That's it. This reminder is your chance to stop, think, and change your behavior. What happens the second time you break the same rule or any other rule in the same day?

Robert: I will stay after class one minute past the bell.

Teacher: And what happens at the third disruption?

Martin: You'll have us stay in class two minutes after the bell.

Continue to go through the hierarchy, discussing corrective actions for breaking rules beyond the third disruption. Be sure to include the severe clause.

Teacher: I have confidence that every one of you can make good decisions about how you behave in school. You know what's expected of you. I want to see you live up to these expectations.

7. **Check for understanding.**

Question students to make sure they understand the corrective actions and how the hierarchy works. Make sure that students understand that these corrective actions will be given every time they choose to misbehave. Students must learn that the corrective actions are inevitable. With this knowledge, they will learn that they are accountable for their actions and have control over the corrective actions by the way they choose to behave.

When you teach your plan, be sure to relate your rules, supportive feedback, and corrective actions to elements that matter in the students' own lives. Students in grades K–3 will respond to home analogies. Students in grades 4–9 will benefit from a discussion that includes peer relationships. High school students can understand expectations in terms of the workplace.

Continual Communication

Post your discipline plan in a prominent spot in the classroom where it will serve as a continuing, helpful reminder of your rules, supportive feedback, and corrective actions.

Send a copy of your classroom discipline plan, along with a letter of explanation, home to parents. Ask parents to review the plan with their children and send a signed portion of the letter back to school. (See Chapter 17 for a sample letter to parents.)

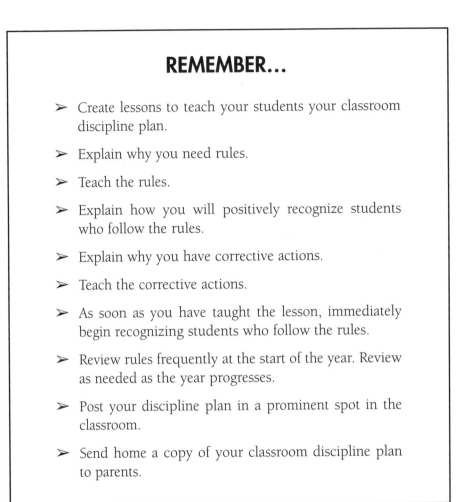

REMEMBER...

➢ Create lessons to teach your students your classroom discipline plan.

➢ Explain why you need rules.

➢ Teach the rules.

➢ Explain how you will positively recognize students who follow the rules.

➢ Explain why you have corrective actions.

➢ Teach the corrective actions.

➢ As soon as you have taught the lesson, immediately begin recognizing students who follow the rules.

➢ Review rules frequently at the start of the year. Review as needed as the year progresses.

➢ Post your discipline plan in a prominent spot in the classroom.

➢ Send home a copy of your classroom discipline plan to parents.

TEACHING RESPONSIBLE BEHAVIOR

Developing your classroom discipline plan and teaching your plan to your students are the first steps toward empowering them to choose the responsible behavior that will enable them to succeed in school. The next step is to teach them how to make responsible behavioral choices in all situations at school.

Chapter 9—Teaching Responsible Behavior:
Part 1—Determining and Teaching Specific Directions

Chapter 10—Teaching Responsible Behavior:
Part 2—Using Supportive Feedback to Motivate Students to Behave

Chapter 11—Teaching Responsible Behavior:
Part 3—Redirecting Nondisruptive Off-Task Behavior
Chapters 9, 10, and 11 discuss a variety of techniques that will help you motivate the majority of your students to behave appropriately.

Chapter 12—Implementing Corrective Actions
Chapter 12 addresses the use of corrective actions within the context of setting firm limits and giving supportive feedback to students.

Chapter 13—Pulling It All Together:
Integrating Behavior Management and Teaching
Finally, you will examine three scenarios in which successful teachers put all these guidelines and techniques together to create a smoothly running classroom in which behavior management efforts are an integral part of the overall teaching process.

Chapter 9

Teaching Responsible Behavior: Part 1—Determining and Teaching Specific Directions

The beginning of the school year is filled with "first times" for students in your classroom.

➤ First time to line up for recess

➤ First time to go to reading or math groups

➤ First time to return to class after lunch

➤ First time to collect and pass out papers

➤ First time to work in a lab situation

➤ First time to work in a cooperative learning group

What happens the first time your students are engaged in any of these activities? Do they know how you expect them to proceed? Do *you* know how you expect them to proceed? Do you give clear directions?

"The first day of school, when the 10 o'clock bell rang, I announced, 'Recess time.' Instead of lining up at the door like I assumed they would,

35 kids stampeded out to the playground. Fortunately, no one was hurt in the rush, but I learned a good lesson about assumptions. I assumed they would line up. They assumed that they could race out the door. We were all mistaken!"

It's important that all your directions are clear if you are going to make the most effective use of your classroom discipline plan. Here's why: Your classroom discipline plan spells out only the general rules of your classroom, the rules that are in effect at all times. You have chosen only a limited number of these rules to be included in your discipline plan. The most important of these rules is "Follow directions." This rule is included to ensure that students promptly follow any direction you might give during the day.

To comply with this rule and meet your expectations, students must understand what each specific direction you give means. You can't assume when you enter into a new activity or procedure anytime during the year that your students will know how to behave the way you want them to.

You would never make this assumption about math competency or reading skills. Likewise, why assume that your behavioral expectations are obvious? After all, every teacher has different ways of moving into groups, collecting work, or distributing assignments. In your classroom, your students need to follow your expectations, not those of another teacher or anyone else.

Right at the beginning of the year, highly successful teachers take time to teach their students exactly how they want them to behave in all classroom situations. They teach and reteach their expectations until every student in the class knows exactly how to handle every single activity or procedure—until all students know how to line up for recess, how to go to learning groups, and how to return to class after lunch.

Teaching specific directions will take time and effort, but the results are worth it. The more time you put in at the beginning of the year teaching directions, the less time you will have to spend repeating the directions as the year goes by. You can actually prevent problems from arising throughout the year by teaching your specific directions at the beginning of the year.

Planning What Directions to Teach

To plan your specific directions, you need to do two things:

1. Identify the instructional settings, routine procedures, and special policies for which specific directions are needed.

2. Determine the specific directions you want your students to follow for each activity and procedure you have identified.

    Take a closer look at these two points.

Identify the instructional settings, routine procedures, and special policies for which you need to determine specific directions.

Examples of Instructional Settings:

➤ Teacher-directed activities

➤ Whole-group discussion

➤ Independent seat work

➤ Sustained silent reading

➤ Independent seat work while teacher is with small group

➤ Small-group activities with teacher

➤ Working in pairs

➤ Taking tests

➤ Cooperative group work

➤ Giving oral reports

➤ Working with special equipment

➤ Working in centers

Examples of Routine Procedures:

➤ Walking to the classroom

➤ Entering the classroom

➤ Leaving the classroom

➤ Beginning the school day

➤ Taking roll

➤ Following attention-getting signal

➤ Lining up

➤ Passing out materials

➤ Collecting papers/homework

➤ Transition from independent seat work to small group

➤ Transition from small group to independent seat work

➤ Getting out books or papers

➤ Emergency drills

➤ End-of-the-day routine

➤ Getting/putting away equipment

➤ Going to the library/lab

Examples of General Policies:

➤ Using drinking fountain

➤ Using pencil sharpener

➤ Going to the restroom

➤ Care of students' desks and chairs

➤ Cleaning up workspace after an activity

➤ Use of materials on bookshelves or in cabinets

➤ Use of computers

➤ Bringing appropriate materials to class

➤ Assigning classwork/homework

➤ Classroom interruptions (phone, visitors, etc.)

Think about a typical week in your own classroom. Start at the beginning of the school day on Monday and work your way through to the end of the day on Friday. Identify the instructional settings, routine procedures, and general policies your students will be engaged in. Try not to leave anything out.

Remember that when you give any direction in class, you're expecting 10, 20, or 30 students to follow it. Don't assume that your behavioral expectations for any activity or procedure are obvious. It's not likely that 30 or more students will instinctively go about following any direction in exactly the same way. You have to tell them exactly what behavior you expect before they will be able to comply.

The time you take to plan your specific directions for all activities and procedures will be more than made up when students are able to follow those directions quickly and without confusion.

Keep in mind that your ultimate goal is not to control behavior but to prepare your students to choose the behavior that will ensure their success in class.

Determine the specific directions you want your students to follow for each activity and procedure.

Teachers have different needs and expectations for their classroom. To set up an environment that works best for you and your students, give thought to your own personal requirements.

"Most of my students this year came from a classroom in which the teacher really didn't mind a lot of noise and moving around. That's fine

for him, but I can't teach that way. I need to know that my classroom will be quiet when I need it to be."

When determining the specific directions you want your students to follow, use these guidelines:

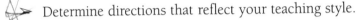 Determine directions that reflect your teaching style.

➤ Create only a limited number of specific directions for each classroom activity.

➤ Make sure your directions are easy for your students to follow. Don't include vague directions such as "act good" or "behave appropriately."

➤ The directions should address student participation, noise level, movement, and materials management desired for the particular activity.

Remember, you are setting up your classroom environment for the year. You must decide how you want your students to behave during each academic activity and routine procedure. Picture each activity and think about each of the directions you would like your students to follow when engaged in the activity.

Participation: What do your want your students to do during each activity?

Should they read by themselves during sustained reading? Should they work with a partner? Should they be engaged in group work?

Noise level: How much noise will you tolerate?

May they talk with each other using 12-inch voices when involved in paired activities? Should there be no talking at all during a test? May your students talk to each other while working on a project?

Movement: What is the level of movement necessary for the activity?

Are they allowed to move from seat to seat during small-group work? May they move freely around the room when working in centers? Do they need to stay seated for the entire activity?

Materials management: How do you want your students to handle their materials?

Are any materials allowed on the desk during a test? Are students responsible for cleaning up their art materials themselves? When are they supposed to sharpen their pencils?

Here are some examples of specific directions that incorporate the guidelines above:

Academic Activity: Teacher-directed lesson in front of the class.

1. Clear your desks of everything but paper and pencil.
   (This direction deals with the desired materials management.)

2. Keep your eyes on me or on your paper. No talking while I'm talking.
   (These directions address the desired noise level.)

3. Raise your hand and wait to be called on to ask or answer a question. Don't shout out answers.
   (These directions deal with the desired student participation.)

Academic Activity: Independent seat work.

1. Have all necessary books, paper, pencils, and other materials on your desk.
   (This direction deals with the desired materials management.)

2. Begin working on your assignment as soon as you receive it.
   (This direction deals with the desired student participation.)

3. Stay in your seat at all times.
   (This direction deals with the desired student movement.)

4. No talking. Raise your hand to ask a question.
   (These directions address the desired noise level.)

Routine Procedure: Entering the classroom.

1. Walk into the room, go directly to your seat, and sit down.
   (This direction deals with the desired student movement.)

2. Get out your materials immediately.
   (This direction deals with the desired materials management.)

3. No talking after the bell rings.
   (This direction deals with the desired noise level.)

Remember that this is your opportunity to create a classroom environment that is conducive to learning and reflects your personal teaching style. Be sure your specific directions reflect your personal needs *and* those of your students. Be creative, be unique, and be specific according to your own wants and needs.

The Difference Between Rules and Directions

➤ Rules are posted in your classroom, and they are in effect at all times during the day.

➤ Directions are in effect for the duration of a specific activity or instructional setting.

➤ Directions may change based on the needs of the teacher and maturity level of the students and the type of learning activity.

Guidelines for Teaching Specific Directions

Teaching specific directions is as important as teaching any academic lesson. Teaching your specific directions ensures that behavior problems will be reduced during all instructional settings, routine procedures, and general policies. Teaching specific directions increases a student's opportunity to succeed at those activities. If your students know what behavior you expect of them, they will be able to comply without any confusion and can focus immediately on the instructional goal of an activity. Your class will run more smoothly and efficiently.

Once you have determined the specific directions you will use, your goal in teaching them is not to simply pass along instructions, but to make this process a learning experience for students as well. Involve students. Don't teach only the *what* and *how;* teach the *why* as well: Teach students why your directions are important to everyone's safety and well-being. When students understand the reasons behind your directions, they will be much more likely to follow them.

You need to prepare before you teach your specific directions.

As in any other kind of lesson, preparation is the key to successful implementation. You will need to prepare a lesson for each direction you will teach. Plan the lesson with the same care as you would plan a lesson for any academic subject. What is your objective? What behavior do you want your students to learn? What specific directions do you want your students to follow? How will you reinforce each lesson?

Plan to teach each specific direction immediately prior to the first time the activity or procedure takes place. This means, of course, that during the first days of school you will be teaching many specific directions for various activities and procedures. Though this may seem like a lot of work, don't let that deter you. The benefits of your efforts will result in reduced behavior problems throughout the year.

Here are two ideas you may want to incorporate into lessons on specific directions:

1. Just as you use visual aids in presenting academic material, it's often a good idea to do the same when you teach directions. A visual reminder will help students focus on your words and remember what you have said. Posters or flipcharts are helpful for older students. Younger nonreaders will benefit from simple drawings on posters. Don't underestimate the value of these reminders for secondary students, either. Everyone needs a reminder now and then. Creating these

visuals will take some time, but it's time you will easily make up as the year proceeds with fewer disruptions. Laminate your charts and plan to use them year after year, updating as necessary.

After you present your lesson, post some of these reminders in the classroom. (Post those directions that students need the most help in remembering or that you feel are most important. Keep them up to date and change as needed.) Giving students visual clues for appropriate behavior will help reinforce your directions. This is a helpful suggestion for students of all ages.

2. It's a good idea to teach students a name for each activity or procedure. The goal of teaching specific directions is for students to make transitions quickly and without confusion or disorder. Therefore, it is important that you are able to communicate each direction as clearly as possible.

   It will be a lot easier for students to move quickly when they hear, for example, "Journal time" than if they hear, "OK, students. Let's spend some time now writing in our journals."

Decide on names for activities and be consistent in their use. These names will serve as cues that students can follow quickly and easily.

Examples:

Seat work	Reading groups
Journal time	SSR (sustained silent reading)
Independent work	Directed lesson
Assembly	Lab groups
Emergency drill	Computer room

Following are some examples of how teachers at different grade levels successfully teach their specific directions. Use the lessons as guidelines for developing a lesson for any specific direction. Keep in mind that your own lessons will differ based on the age of your students and the directions you are teaching, but the focus of explanation, teaching, and checking for understanding remains the same.

Each lesson covers the following sequence:

1. Explain the rationale for the directions.

2. Involve the students by asking questions (for younger students).

3. Explain the specific directions.

4. Check for understanding.

Grades K–3: Teaching Specific Directions

With students in grades K–3, you will want to spend plenty of time teaching and reinforcing each specific direction. Give students the opportunity to role-play the directions, and provide ample opportunities to follow the directions after the lesson is given. Reteach and reinforce often. Use pictures or other visual clues to help reinforce the directions.

Specific Directions for Responding to the Teacher's Signal for Attention

1. **Explain the rationale for the directions.**

    Teacher: There will be times during the day when I'm going to need all of you to stop what you're doing and give me your complete attention—times when I will need to know that everyone is listening to me.

    When I need everyone's attention, I am going to give you a signal—for example, ringing a bell or turning a flashlight on and off.

2. **Involve the students by asking questions.**

    Teacher: When are some of the times that I will need to use a signal in class? When is it important that I get your attention?

Students: When we need to stop one activity and start another. When it's time to clean up. When you have an important idea you want to tell us.

Teacher: Those are all excellent reasons. And I think you can see why I will need to use a signal. A signal lets everyone know that it's time to stop what you're doing and pay attention to me.

3. **Explain the specific directions.**

Explain the signal that will be used.

Teacher: When I want your attention, I will ring this small bell. When I give this signal, I want you to do three things.

➤ Stop whatever you're doing.

➤ Look at me.

➤ Listen to me.

Stop, look, and listen. Don't turn around to your neighbor. Don't move around the room. Wait for me to give directions.

4. **Check for understanding.**

Check for understanding by asking several students to restate the direction. Reinforce the directions by writing them on the board. With K–1 students, you might instead show a poster showing a stop sign (stop), an eye (look), and an ear (listen).

Teacher: Now, who can raise a hand and tell me what you are to do first when I ring the bell?

As students state the directions, write them on the board. Next, have the students practice or role-play the directions.

Teacher: Let's see how well you have learned this signal. Right now we're going to practice what you will do when I give the signal. I want all of you to stand up and wiggle. (*Students comply.*)

When I give the signal, I expect you to stop, look, and listen. That means, stop wiggling, look at me, and listen to me. All right. Start wiggling.

Students begin wiggling. In a few minutes, give the signal by ringing the bell. Begin immediately to acknowledge those students who are following the direction.

Teacher: Marcia has stopped wiggling. Bob has his eyes on me. Pat is listening. Well done!

Now, does anyone have any questions about how to follow my signal?

Grades 4–6: Teaching Specific Directions

Students in grades 4–6 want to understand the reasons behind the directions they are expected to follow. Explain why they need to follow each direction and what the benefit will be for them and the other students.

Specific Directions for a Seat Work Activity

1. **Explain the rationale for the directions.**

Teacher: During the year, I am often going to ask you to do work at your desk. I call this seat work. Doing seat work means working on your own at your desk. You may be reading. You may be writing. You may be working on a math problem. Whatever it is that you will be doing, you will be doing it on your own.

To make sure you understand exactly how I expect you to behave during seat work, I am going to teach you the directions I expect you to follow. It's important that everyone follows these directions because everyone needs to be able to work in a quiet environment.

2. **Explain the specific directions.**

Teacher: I have listed the directions for seat work here. *(Point to chart.)* Let's look at the first one. When I tell you it's time for seat work, I expect you first to put all necessary books, paper, pencils, and other materials you will need on your desk. I also expect you to clear your desk of any other materials you won't be using.

Now let's look at the second direction. *(Point to the second direction on chart.)* "Stay in your seat and begin working on your own as soon as you receive the assignment." That means no wandering around. No working on other classwork. No reading a library book.

The third direction for seat work is *(Point to chart)* "If you need help or want to ask a question, raise your hand." I will come over to you or ask you to come to my desk.

Finally, the fourth direction *(Point to chart)* is "No talking during seat work." Seat work is quiet time.

3. **Check for understanding.**

Teacher: Now, I want to make sure that I was very clear in explaining these directions for seat work and that everyone understands what I expect of you. Can someone raise a hand and tell me, in your own words, what I mean by the first direction, "Have all necessary materials on your desk"?

Julio: You mean that we have to take out all of the stuff we'll need for doing the assignment, like paper, and pencils, and books, and put them on our desks.

Teacher: You did a good job of listening. Can someone explain the next direction *(Point to chart),* "Stay in your seat and begin working on your assignment on your own as soon as you receive it"?

Bella: That means we need to begin working as soon as we get the assignment. You can't get up and talk to your friends.

Teacher: Exactly right! Can someone now explain what I mean by this direction *(Point to third direction),* "If you have a question or need help, raise your hand and wait until the teacher calls on you"?

Bella: That means that if you don't understand the assignment, or if you need help on a problem or something, you should raise your hand and wait for the teacher to call your name. Then the teacher will either come to your desk or you will go up to hers.

Teacher: Do any of you have questions about what I want you to do when you are doing seat work?

Roberto: What if I need a sharp pencil?

Teacher: If you need to get a sharpened pencil, raise your dull pencil in the air. When I give you permission, you may place your pencil in the "dull" pencil cup and take a sharpened pencil from the cup marked "sharpened." Then return immediately to your seat and begin working.

Grades 7–12: Teaching Specific Directions

Teach your specific directions in a matter-of-fact manner to students in grades 7–12. Make it clear to them why you expect these directions to be followed.

Specific Directions for a Directed Lesson

1. **Explain the rationale for the directions.**

   Teacher: When I'm speaking in front of the class, I need you to behave in a way that I can teach and everyone can learn. For that reason, I'm going to tell you exactly how I expect you to behave during a lecture.

2. **Explain the specific directions.**

   Teacher: These are the directions I expect you to follow when I'm speaking.

   ➤ Clear your desks of everything but paper and pencil.

   I don't want anything out except paper for taking notes and a pencil to write with.

   ➤ Eyes on me, or eyes on your paper.

   During a lecture, you need to be either looking at me or looking at your paper as you write. Eyes on me. Eyes on your paper.

   ➤ Raise your hand and wait to be called on to ask or answer a question.

   If you want to ask me a question, answer a question, or respond to something another student has said, you need to raise your hand.

3. **Check for understanding.**

   Teacher: Who can tell me what I expect you to do during a lecture?

   Ask for volunteers to restate directions.

   Immediately follow up any specific direction lesson with the activity or procedure that has just been taught. Be sure to recognize students who follow the directions appropriately, and provide reminders (or reteach if necessary) to those students who don't.

Need for Review

Depending on the age and ability of your students, you may find it necessary to review specific directions occasionally, especially at the beginning of the school year or just before an activity that the students haven't participated in for a while.

At the beginning of the school year, review the directions each time you engage in a different routine procedure or instructional setting. As the year proceeds, you will know when you need to review. The review procedure can be as simple as going over the directions or asking students to state the rules aloud for the rest of the class.

Guidelines for Reviewing Specific Directions

First two weeks:	Review directions each time the class engages in the activity.
First month:	Review directions each Monday (as a reminder and refresher for the week to come).
Remainder of year:	Review directions as needed. It is especially important to review directions after a vacation, on special days when students are especially keyed up (the first snowfall, Halloween, field-trip day), or whenever the class engages in a new activity.

REMEMBER...

➤ Don't assume that students know how you want them to behave in all situations that occur during a regular school day. You need to teach your expectations.

➤ Identify the classroom situations for which specific directions are needed. Then determine those directions.

➤ Teach your specific directions immediately prior to the first time the activity takes place.

➤ Teach the lesson with the same care as you would any academic lesson.

➤ Explain your rationale for teaching each direction.

➤ Explain the directions.

➤ Check for understanding.

➤ Review the specific directions for each activity as long as is necessary.

➤ Post visual clues (charts, posters, illustrations) around the classroom to help remind students of appropriate behavior during different activities and procedures.

Chapter 10

Teaching Responsible Behavior: Part 2—Using Supportive Feedback to Motivate Students to Behave

Now that you have determined directions for each classroom situation and have taught those directions to your class, your goal is to help students achieve success in following those directions. Supportive feedback of a student's appropriate behavior is the most effective way to achieve this goal. If you recognize a student's compliance with your directions, the student will be motivated to repeat his performance in order to be recognized again. Over time, however, the student will internalize the rules and no longer need your supportive feedback to comply. He will have learned to manage his behavior on his own.

Guidelines for Providing Supportive Feedback

This chapter presents supportive feedback techniques that will help you teach your students to choose to behave responsibly. The focus is on three areas:

1. Using behavioral narration to motivate students to get on task

2. Using supportive approaches to keep students on task

3. Implementing classwide reward systems

Let's take a closer look at each of these techniques.

Use behavioral narration to motivate students to get on task.

During the course of the day, you will be giving your students many different directions. You have taught your students your specific directions, but experience has shown you that some of your students still may not follow them.

When students do not comply with specific directions, teachers often focus immediately on students who aren't doing what they should be doing.

"Seth, get back to your seat and start working on your assignment. Stop acting silly."

"Carol, stop talking to your neighbor. Get back to work."

"Jaime, put your math book away and get out your social studies book. You're wasting time!"

The teacher focuses on the negative, pointing out the students who are misbehaving. Students who do meet expectations are generally ignored.

This kind of response creates a negative environment in the classroom. It sends the message to students that the teacher is looking for misbehavior, is expecting misbehavior, and is ready and waiting to pounce on students who don't follow directions.

Students get the impression that the best way to attract attention is by engaging in inappropriate behavior.

This is not the message you want to communicate. A more successful approach would be to keep the emphasis on the positive by looking for compliance with your rules. Acknowledge students who are doing what they are supposed to do. This technique is called *behavioral narration*.

The teacher gives a direction as follows:

"Everybody please line up for recess."

Now she immediately looks for students who are following directions and points out their actions by narrating their appropriate behavior.

"Andrew is lining up quietly. Ellen is in line, too."

Negative focus or positive? Which kind of response is more motivating to students? Which fills the room with positive energy? Which response is less stressful for the teacher to make and students to receive? Most importantly, which response focuses the other students' attention on the appropriate behavior?

You have a choice. You can focus on negative behavior, or you can redirect that behavior by focusing on students who are engaged in positive behavior.

Look for what's working in your classroom and acknowledge it. It's simply a matter of viewing your classroom activities in a positive rather than a negative light. Using the behavioral narration technique will assist you in reaching that goal. Here's how it works:

1. Give a direction.

2. Immediately look for at least two students who are following the direction.

3. Say the students' names and narrate their behavior as they are following the direction.

This technique reinforces students who are following your directions, and reminds those who are not yet following them of what they are supposed to do without reprimanding them directly. Students who are able to quickly follow your directions become models for the students who need more time to process your instructions. These students have the opportunity to *hear* you narrate the correct behavior and *see* their classmates appropriately engaged. Behavioral narration, therefore, supports a variety of learning styles and is especially helpful to students who are visual learners or students who tend to daydream in class.

Here are examples of behavioral narration in action:

Direction: Take your places on the reading mat.

Behavioral narration:	Mariko and Danny are already at their places on the reading mat.
Direction:	Line up quickly without talking.
Behavioral narration:	Debbie lined up quickly without talking. Richard is in line without talking, too.
Direction:	Eyes on me and no talking, please.
Behavioral narration:	Jeff has his eyes on me. Carlos is sitting and not talking.

A note to teachers of older students: With adolescents, such overt comments in front of their peers can backfire. For many adolescents, nothing is more embarrassing than to be singled out for being "good." One way around this dilemma is for you to pair your behavioral narration with a reward that benefits the entire class. This concept combines behavioral narration with a classwide reward system.

A classwide reward system is typically a point system that enables the entire class to earn a reward, such as one night with no homework. This concept will be discussed in detail later in this chapter.

Below is an example of an eighth grade teacher who is using a classwide reward system to help teach his students to go to their cooperative learning groups.

"When you go to your small groups, I want you to take your assignment, walk quietly, sit down with your group, and start your assignment.

"Marco's walking quietly. Yumi has her assignment. She's seated and ready to go. That's a point for the class toward free time. We have 18 points. Two more and you get a homework-free night."

Harness the power that's in your classroom. Peer pressure is a very compelling force, particularly with older students. Use it to your advantage.

Frequency of Use

How often should you use behavioral narration?

At the beginning of the year, you are creating a safe classroom environment based on cooperation, caring, and trust. You will be placing a heavy emphasis on teaching students how to comply with your classroom rules to create this environment. Therefore, in the beginning you will have to use supportive feedback techniques such as behavioral narration quite frequently. The more you need to teach children how to behave, the more you need to use verbal recognition. Remember that the goal of supportive feedback is to start strong, then gradually decrease its frequency.

Guidelines for Frequency of Behavioral Narration

Weeks 1–2:	Use behavioral narration every time you give a direction. Don't worry about overdoing it.
Weeks 2–4:	Use behavioral narration every third time you give a direction.
After first month:	Use behavioral narration every fourth or fifth time you give a direction. Maintain this frequency level throughout the year.

Your goal should be to acknowledge each student every day. Behavioral narration can help you reach this goal easily and without a lot of extra thought. Think of it this way: You may give 100 directions a day. If you acknowledge a student with every fourth or fifth direction, you will be recognizing students about 25 times a day.

Use supportive approaches to keep students on task.

You have learned how behavioral narration can guide students to follow directions and *get* on task. Now, how can you help students *stay* on task so you can maximize their learning?

The best—and easiest—way to build responsible student behavior is to provide frequent supportive feedback. In other words, don't stop recognizing your students once they are on task. Keep it up. Let students know that you notice and appreciate their good work. Give them the encouragement they need to maintain their progress.

Verbal Recognition

Unfortunately, using frequent supportive feedback doesn't come naturally to all teachers. Most have to work hard to develop the habit of acknowledging and supporting their students to stay on track. Training yourself to use supportive feedback *before* providing a corrective action will have enormous payoff. You can develop this habit by continually monitoring the class and by providing frequent verbal recognition to those who are on task. Here's an example of a teacher using consistent verbal support integrated with teaching a lesson:

Teacher: Which group was able to come up with a solution to this math problem? I am looking for students with their hands up and waiting to be called on.

Many students raise their hands. Several mumble or shout out answers. The teacher focuses on Kelly, who has her hand raised and is not speaking.

Teacher: Kelly, how did your group solve it?

Kelly responds.

Teacher: That's one way to solve the problem. And Kelly, raising your hand and waiting quietly was exactly the right thing to do. Did any group approach the problem in a different way?

120

The teacher again watches for students who have their hands raised and are not speaking out.

Teacher: Yes, Robert?

Robert shares how his group solved the problem.

Teacher: Now we have two different methods that work. And Robert, you raised your hand and waited for me to call on you. Well done! Let's see if there's a third solution to this problem.

Chris responds.

Teacher: Great answer, Chris. And I see that most of you are remembering to raise your hands and wait to be called on before you answer.

You can see in this example that the teacher was doing more than just teaching math. She was also teaching students how to behave appropriately in a specific situation. By recognizing those students who raised their hands and waited to be called on before speaking, she reinforced her specific direction for this activity. However, her verbal recognition not only encouraged Kelly, Robert, and Chris to cooperate and stay involved with the lesson, but influenced the entire class as well. By integrating behavior management into her teaching routine, this teacher will ensure that her lessons teach more than just a particular subject. Her lessons also teach cooperation.

Here are some guidelines for using verbal recognition:

➤ **Verbal recognition should be personal.**
When using verbal recognition, always include the student's name. Let students know that your words are directed at them, and that they made a great effort.

This is especially important when you are recognizing the behavior of a student who is across the room. A statement such as "Thank you for working quietly back there" is not as effective as "Jack and Sally are working quietly. Keep up the good work!"

➤ **Verbal recognition must be genuine.**
To be convincing to students, to show that you really mean what you say, be genuinely appreciative of appropriate behavior. Insincere comments are no form of recognition at all.

➤ **Verbal recognition is descriptive and specific.**
"Miranda is walking quietly in line. Great, Miranda." "You went right to work, Simon. Terrific!" Being specific about the student's behavior increases the likelihood that the appropriate behavior will be repeated. Avoid evaluative comments such as "I like the way you are working." They're not as effective as descriptive, specific statements because the student focuses on whether the teacher likes him rather than on whether his behavior is appropriate.

Descriptive Verbal Recognition	Vague Verbal Recognition
"Sue is lined up ready for recess. Good work, Sue."	"You're so good, Sue."
"You did a great job outlining your essay, Victor."	"Nice job, Victor."
"You were very careful putting the books away, Kerry."	"I like the way you're helping, Kerry."

➤ **Verbal recognition should be age-appropriate.**
You cannot acknowledge a kindergarten student the same way you would a high school student. Here are some guidelines:

Grades K–3: Young children want your approval publicly. Public approval increases their self-esteem. They want to please you, and it means a lot to them to know that you approve of their actions. Thus, your positive statements to your students should reflect the fact that you, their teacher, noticed the good behavior. Your students then become models for the rest of the class.

> *"I see you went all morning without talking out, Kirby! Class, let's give a hand to Kirby."*

> *"Danilo, you put a lot of work into your science project. The posters you painted are so interesting. I love them! You should feel proud of your hard work."*

Grades 4–6: As students mature, your approval of their actions is still important, but it becomes more important that they feel good about themselves. Pride and self-esteem are internalized. Your acknowledgment needs to reflect this shift in attitude.

> *"You went all morning without shouting out, Tamara. You really learned to control yourself."*

> *"Earl, your science project reflects a lot of research on your part. All your work paid off. This is an excellent presentation!"*

Grades 7–12: The key to making effective positive comments to adolescents is to say it in a simple, matter-of-fact manner. The simpler, the better. Your acknowledgment may also be appreciated more by older students if it is given privately rather than in front of the entire class.

> *"You were quiet all period, Joseph. Great improvement."*

> *"Excellent project, Kim. It gave me a lot to think about."*

Scanning

A common behavior problem, particularly at the beginning of the year, is keeping students working independently.

The scanning technique is useful when you are working with a small group of students or with an individual student, while the rest of the class is working independently. By using this technique, you can keep independent workers on task and continue working with one small group.

The objective of this technique is to encourage students who are on task to remain on task. This technique will help you recognize students who normally may not receive attention until they misbehave.

Here's how to use the scanning technique:

When you are working with a small group, look up every few minutes and scan the students who are working independently. As you notice students who are working appropriately, take a moment to recognize their good behavior.

"David is working quietly on his math. Keep up the good work, David."

The student will appreciate the recognition and continue working independently. Other students will get the message that you are aware of what's going on in the room, and they will be motivated to stay on task as well.

Here's an example of how scanning is used when a teacher is working with a small reading group and the rest of the class is working independently:

Teacher: All right, Doug. Please read from the top of page 83.

Doug reads the paragraph.

Teacher: You read with such expression, Doug!

The teacher looks up, scans the class, and sees that Yvette is busily at work on her assignment. The teacher takes the opportunity to recognize Yvette's effort.

Teacher: Yvette, it looks like you're working hard on your report.

Yvette looks up, smiles, and continues her work. Other students look up also and then focus back on their assignments.

How often you use the scanning technique will depend on your students' age and level of motivation. At the beginning of the year, remind students of their expected behavior by using verbal recognition while scanning often. Later in the year, you may not want to interrupt on-task behavior, not even with a positive statement. But no matter how you use this technique, scanning demonstrates to students that you are always aware of their appropriate behavior, even when you are not working directly with them.

Circulating the Classroom

While students are working independently, circulate throughout the room and give supportive feedback. One on one, you can always let a student know that you recognize his appropriate behavior. This is a particularly effective technique with secondary students.

> *"Mike, you remained focused on your work the entire period. You finished the entire assignment!"*

You also may want to give a student general acknowledgment for how she is behaving.

> *"Taylor, you are very cooperative today. You are getting along very well with everyone."*

Circulating among your students lets them know that you're reachable. You're there, available to help when they need you.

There is no reason to phase out this technique. Keep it going strong all year long. Don't stay seated behind your desk. Use independent work time to your advantage and strengthen your relationship with your students. Move among them, make yourself available for questions, boost their self-esteem through acknowledgment and positive support. Each time you circulate the classroom, you have an opportunity to show your students that you notice their good efforts. You have the opportunity to show them that you notice something special about them. It will let them know that you care.

This technique is especially helpful to provide consistent and meaningful supportive feedback to adolescents. Adolescents accept verbal recognition more readily when given in private. Thus, circulating the room during independent work time is the ideal opportunity to stay in touch with them.

"Whenever my students are working independently, whether alone or in groups, I take the opportunity to do some 'esteem boosting.' While the kids are busy, I don't sit down and I don't grade papers. As they work, I roam around the classroom. I might stop by one student's desk, lean down, and quietly acknowledge his work.

"To another student I might mention what a nice-looking shirt he is wearing. To still another I might jot a quick positive note for her to take home to her parents.

"The point is, I stay in touch with a word, a smile, a personal comment. Working the room helps keep the students on task, and it gives me an opportunity for some one-on-one contact.

"In 10 minutes I can let 6 to 10 students know—unobtrusively and naturally—that I care about them."

Putting Names on the Board for Good Behavior

Make an additional effort to acknowledge students who are behaving. It's a great way to back up the verbal recognition you give.

One motivating way to encourage younger students to behave is to simply write their names on the board when you notice appropriate behavior. Designate a corner of the blackboard as "Classroom Superstars Corner." Play a game of "How many names can we get on the board today?" Set a goal to put at least 20 names on the board each day. Erase the names at the end of the day and start anew the next day.

Implement classwide reward systems.

The previous techniques used verbal recognition to motivate individual students to behave appropriately. In addition, you can use classwide reward systems to augment your individual reinforcement efforts.

Here's an example:

A first grade teacher was the consummate master at using Marbles in a Jar to motivate students. She used this classwide reward system to help teach students her behavioral expectations at the beginning of the year, and she used it throughout the year when her students needed reminders to follow her directions.

On the first day of school, she always kept marbles and a jar close at hand, ready to use. Her goal was to use the marbles continually to reinforce the students for following directions. First she would set an easy goal for the students to reach. Thirty marbles in the jar would typically earn the class free time. And within the first day she would see to it that the students would earn the reward. More important was the combination of the clink of the marbles with words of acknowledgment, such as "Good job following directions." Her students were learning in a positive manner how to follow her directions. And the technique didn't take away much time at all from her efforts to teach subject matter.

After a few days, she increased the number of marbles needed to earn free time. By the end of the second week of school, the marbles were no longer needed. The students had learned to follow her directions, quickly get on task, and stay on task.

Throughout the year, whenever a problem developed, the marbles reappeared.

This classwide recognition system was particularly helpful on "high disruption" days: the first snowfall, the first day back at school after winter vacation, and the last few days before vacation.

By using the Marbles in a Jar technique, this teacher was able to encourage students to behave responsibly and appropriately in a positive and enjoyable manner, without having to rely on threats or corrective actions to motivate her students to behave.

Here's another example of a classwide reward system in action:

A middle-school English teacher had a very active, very social seventh grade class. These students always seemed to prefer clowning around to settling down to work. Acknowledging students who were on task, even one on one, proved ineffective. He found he had to use corrective actions more and more frequently, and the classroom became an increasingly negative environment for all.

To counteract this deteriorating situation, he instituted a classwide recognition system. Whenever he caught a student on task, that student earned a point for the entire class. Fifty points would earn a night of no homework. The students quickly became motivated to reach the goal. They were so motivated that they would often verbally remind each other. Comments like "Shhh," "Cool it," or "Be quiet!" would often come from the students themselves before the teacher even had a chance to correct the off-task student himself. Within a week, the points were earned. The teacher kept the point system in place for the next three weeks. By the end of the third week, the students' behavior was more controlled, learning had increased, and the students had accepted that following their teacher's directions was necessary to have a cooperative and positive work environment.

This is a particularly effective technique to use with older students. Rather than the teacher controlling the students' behavior, the students employ peer pressure to monitor each other. As a result, they internalize the classroom rules, which is a very important and necessary first step to student self-management.

Increasing Your Consistency in Giving Supportive Feedback

It's not easy to maintain a high frequency of supportive feedback in the classroom. Most of us don't do it naturally. Here is a suggestion for some highly effective techniques that will help ensure more frequent verbal recognition.

Have a P.R. (Positive Reminder) plan.

Don't let supportive feedback slip your mind, even for a moment. The following ideas will keep a positive word on the tip of your tongue all day long.

1. **Post classroom reminders.**
   How many times a day do you glance at the classroom clock? Now you can get more than just the time of day. Hang a "Catch them being

good" reminder on the wall right next to the clock. This note will give you a nudge throughout the day and remind you to keep looking for positive behavior to reinforce.

2. **Put reminders in lesson plans.**
    Your lesson-plan book is a great place to jot down reminders to yourself. Make a note that in addition to teaching subject matter, you will also acknowledge students for appropriate behavior. Use a fluorescent marking pen to highlight the idea.

3. **Set specific goals for the frequency of your supportive feedback.**
    Goals help give direction and structure to one's efforts. Each day in your lesson-plan book, write your goals for delivering supportive feedback.

    "I will write 20 students' names on the board for behaving appropriately."

    "I will send home two positive notes per day per class."

    "Each class will earn 10 classwide points per period."

As you go through the school day, always keep in mind that the goal of a successful teacher is to recognize the appropriate behavior of every student at least once a day. It will show them that you care and that you are there for them if they need you.

Supportive feedback will make students feel good about themselves. When students feel good about themselves, when they feel confident about what they are doing, their self-esteem rises. Self-esteem is perhaps the most important ingredient for behavioral and academic success.

REMEMBER...

➤ Use behavioral narration to reinforce students who are following directions and to give a positively stated reminder to those who are not yet following the directions.

➤ Use verbal recognition to encourage students to continue appropriate behavior.

➤ Use verbal recognition to increase a student's self-esteem.

➤ Use verbal recognition to reduce behavioral problems and create a more positive classroom environment.

➤ Use the scanning technique when you are working with a small group of students while the rest of the class is working independently.

➤ As you teach, circulate throughout the classroom to recognize your students individually.

➤ Recognize younger students for good behavior by writing their names on the board as a "Classroom Superstar!"

➤ Set a goal to acknowledge every student every day.

➤ Use a classwide recognition system to motivate your class to work toward a specific behavioral goal.

➤ Integrate consistent verbal recognition into any lesson and any communication with students.

Chapter 11

Teaching Responsible Behavior: Part 3—Redirecting Nondisruptive Off-Task Behavior

B y teaching your rules and specific directions, and by providing consistent supportive feedback to your students, you are going to eliminate the vast majority of problems before they begin.

But realistically, no matter how clearly you teach your expectations, and no matter how supportive you are, there will be students who engage in behavior that is not in their best interest. It is behavior that doesn't enhance self-esteem and doesn't promote success in school. It is behavior that frustrates you or causes you to feel stressed at the end of the day. It is behavior that creates a negative classroom environment.

This behavior can take two forms: disruptive off-task behavior and nondisruptive off-task behavior.

Disruptive off-task behavior means a student is keeping you from teaching and other students from learning. Because it is so obtrusive, disruptive behavior is easy to recognize. You will learn how to deal with this type of behavior in Chapter 12.

Typical disruptive off-task behaviors are:

➤ Shouting out in class

➤ Throwing paper or other objects

➤ Pushing or shoving another student

➤ Running in the classroom

➤ Talking back

Nondisruptive off-task behavior is not always as easy to identify or respond to. This kind of behavior describes a student who is not disturbing others but is not paying attention or following directions either. The student is physically in the classroom, but attentively, the seat is vacant.

Typical nondisruptive off-task behaviors are:

➤ Looking out the window

➤ Reading instead of listening

➤ Doodling instead of working

➤ Working on an assignment from another class

➤ Daydreaming or sleeping with head down on desk

In this chapter, you will learn how to handle nondisruptive off-task behavior.

Ineffective Responses to Nondisruptive Off-Task Behavior

Welcome to the gray zone of behavior management: Your classroom appears to be running smoothly. No one is disrupting, except you notice one of your students is not really participating. He is sitting quietly, but he is looking out the window, or his head is down on his desk.

What can be done to guide this student back into classroom activity? Should you do anything?

Here's how many teachers deal with nondisruptive off-task behavior:

1. They ignore the problem.

2. They give an immediate, sometimes harsh, corrective action.

Let's examine the effect each of these responses has on the situation.

Ignoring the Problem

Sometimes teachers continue lecturing or giving instructions even when it is obvious that some students are paying no attention. These teachers are ignoring inappropriate behavior. It may be unintentional, but these teachers are, in effect, condoning behavior that is not in their students' best interest. They're telling their students, "In my class it's OK not to pay attention. It's OK to look out the window while I'm speaking. In my class it's OK not to learn." In a way, these teachers are communicating to their students that they don't care enough about them to make sure that they do learn.

That is not the message you want to send to any of your students.

Nondisruptive off-task behavior hurts the students engaged in that behavior. As a professional, it's your job and your responsibility to teach each and every student. Nondisruptive off-task behavior is unacceptable because it is detrimental to a student's success. It must not be ignored.

Don't give any of your students license to avoid learning. Don't let any of your students become shadows in your classroom. Take the time to keep them involved and attentive in your classroom. Make the effort to get them interested in your lessons and keep them interested.

Issuing an Immediate Corrective Action

You're teaching a lesson. Everything seems to be going fine. Students are quiet and seem to be paying attention. Then you see Jason slouching in his chair, staring out the window. Your instant reaction is: "Jason, sit up and listen! You have just lost recess today!"

Controlling your students' nondisruptive off-task behavior with immediate corrective actions is not the answer. Many times such a harsh response will often alienate potentially enthusiastic students rather than get them back on task and involved in the class you are teaching.

You must make sure that you recognize nondisruptive off-task behavior for what it is: a momentary lapse of attention. It needs to be redirected calmly, and with care and understanding.

Effective Responses to Nondisruptive Behavior

The teachers who deal most successfully with nondisruptive off-task behavior do so with a variety of techniques, which are neatly woven into their style of teaching. They never miss a beat. There's neither alarm in their voice nor anger in their response. In a manner that doesn't stop them from teaching or raise their stress level, they remain in control and continue with their lesson plans.

Redirect students back on task.

Here are four techniques used to redirect nondisruptive off-task behavior.

Redirecting Technique #1: The "Look"
Communicate that you are aware of and disapprove of the behavior with a firm but calm look. Make sure you establish eye contact.

> *Instead of doing his assignment, Devon rocks back and forth in his chair. Noticing Devon's off-task behavior, the teacher makes direct eye contact with him, looking straight at him with a firm, calm expression on her face. She maintains eye contact until he puts all four legs of his chair on the floor and gets back to his assignment.*

Redirecting Technique #2: Physical Proximity
Redirect a student back on task by walking over and standing close by. The student will know why you have arrived at her side and she will respond. You can continue teaching and not miss a beat.

> *While leading a discussion, the teacher notices that Shannon put her head down and "tuned out." The teacher walks to the back of the room*

to Shannon's seat and stands near her desk while continuing to instruct the class.

With this action the teacher clearly and firmly communicated to the student that her behavior was inappropriate.

Redirecting Technique #3: Mention the Off-Task Student's Name While Teaching

Just mentioning a student's name while you are teaching a lesson may be enough to redirect his attention back on task.

While at the board, the teacher notices that Tanya and Michael are off task and not paying attention. The teacher, in a matter-of-fact manner, continues the lesson saying, "I want all of you, including Tanya and Michael, to come up with the answer to this problem." As soon as their names are mentioned, Tanya and Michael immediately begin paying attention.

Redirecting Technique #4: Proximity Praise

Another way to redirect a student back on task is to focus on the appropriate behavior of those students around him.

The entire class, with the exception of John, is working on their assignments. On either side of John, Nolan and Cindy are both following directions and doing their work. Wanting to get John on task, the teacher says, "Nolan and Cindy are following directions and working on their assignments."

As she expects, John looks around him, notices what is going on, and gets back to work.

This technique actually allows you to achieve two goals. You communicate to the student in a supportive way that you're aware that he's not doing his work, and that you want him back on task. At the same time, you are giving verbal acknowledgment to those students who are on task.

Each of the four redirecting techniques presented here does not interrupt the flow of your teaching. Using these techniques results in a winning situation for everyone: You can keep teaching and the off-task student resumes learning. You prevent potentially disruptive behavior before it even begins.

Once a student is back on track, acknowledge him.

Don't forget to recognize the student's appropriate behavior. Take advantage of the opportunity to acknowledge his behavior. It will show the student that you corrected his behavior because you care too much about him to allow him to fall through the cracks. And it will make him feel good about having made the choice to pay attention to your teaching.

If Redirection Doesn't Work

By now you may be thinking, *It all sounds easy here on the pages of a book, but in my class some of those off-task students will go right back off task a few minutes later. How many times do I redirect them before I start giving corrective actions?*

That's an important question. Redirecting off-task behavior is a good technique that gives students an opportunity to get back to work. But you can't bend over backward, either. Nondisruptive off-task behavior can't be allowed to continue. If it does, it becomes disruptive.

You want to prevent disruptive behavior. You cannot allow the student to get into a pattern of failure.

Here's a rule of thumb: If you find yourself having to redirect a student three times a day (elementary) or two times a class period (secondary), you can assume that the student is not receiving enough structure to help him control his behavior. In these situations, turn to your disciplinary hierarchy and issue a reminder. If the off-task behavior continues even after that, you may need to use corrective actions from your disciplinary hierarchy. In the next chapter, you will learn how to implement corrective actions.

If the behavior seems out of character for that student, perhaps something is wrong that causes him to tune out. You need to use your own judgment in determining whether the particular student should progress through your disciplinary hierarchy as usual. You may have to exercise leniency and understanding until you find out why your usually attentive student seems so absentminded. Talk to the student after class and ask, "Is there something I can do? Let's talk." Always remember that your own good judgment is your most valuable tool in assessing a student's behavior.

REMEMBER...

➤ Differentiate between disruptive off-task behavior and nondisruptive off-task behavior. Nondisruptive off-task behavior is behavior in which a student is not disturbing others but is not paying attention or following directions either.

➤ Don't ignore nondisruptive off-task behavior. It's not in your students' best interest.

➤ Rather than provide a corrective action or ignore the behavior, redirect the behavior.

➤ Redirect a student's nondisruptive off-task behavior while you continue teaching.

➤ Give the student a "look" that says you are aware of and disapprove of his behavior.

➤ Stand by an off-task student's side as you teach.

➤ Mention the off-task student's name while teaching.

➤ Use proximity praise to redirect an off-task student.

➤ As soon as a student is back on task, take the first opportunity to acknowledge his appropriate behavior.

➤ If redirecting is not effective, it may be appropriate to provide corrective actions from your discipline hierarchy.

Chapter 12

Implementing Corrective Actions

Simply planning corrective actions and teaching them to your students is not going to be sufficient to motivate all students to behave. You will have to follow through when they disrupt. Remember that actions speak louder than words.

In Chapter 7 you learned to develop a discipline hierarchy as part of your classroom discipline plan. How you use the corrective actions in the hierarchy will determine its success in helping you motivate students to choose responsible behavior.

Students need to learn that corrective actions are a natural outcome of misbehavior. The key is not the corrective action itself, but the inevitability that an action will be taken each time a rule is broken or a direction is not followed—not just sometimes, not every now and then, but every single time.

Corrective actions given consistently and calmly help teach students to behave responsibly. The consistent use of corrective actions teaches students that if they choose to behave in an inappropriate manner, they will also choose to accept the consequences of that choice.

To successfully manage a classroom, there must be a balance between giving supportive feedback and providing corrective actions. Students will not respect your supportive feedback unless it is backed up with firm limits. And limits will be ineffective unless staying within those limits is reinforced by your acknowledgment of their appropriate behavior. Both are key elements in a caring relationship.

Guidelines for Using Corrective Actions

Here are the basic guidelines to follow to ensure that your use of corrective actions will help students choose responsible behavior.

Provide corrective actions in a calm, matter-of-fact manner.

How you provide corrective actions to students is as important as the actions themselves. Too many teachers become frustrated and angry when students disrupt, and their responses reflect this frustration.

Here's an example:

In a seventh grade class, Kirk and Stephen begin talking and laughing while a study team is giving a group report. Kirk and Stephen receive a reminder. As the study team resumes the presentation, Kirk and Stephen once again begin disrupting.

Teacher: *(In an angry tone of voice)* Kirk, Stephen, there you go again being rude and inconsiderate. I've had it with your immature behavior. You can just cut it out right now. I will see you both after class!

Stay calm. Getting angry and demeaning students is counterproductive. Corrective actions are not meant to punish students. They are intended to stop the disruptive behavior and to remind the students that it is in their own interest to choose more appropriate behavior. Therefore, all you need to do is calmly but firmly tell your disruptive students what they are supposed to do, followed by mentioning the corrective action they will receive.

Here's how that situation should have been handled:

Teacher: *(Calmly)* Kirk and Stephen, this is not the time to be talking and laughing. You need to be listening. You have chosen to stay one minute after class.

Be consistent. Provide a corrective action every time students choose to disrupt.

Here's an example of consistency in action:

Students in a sixth grade class are working independently. One student, Jean, turns around and starts scribbling on Bert's paper. Bert says, "Stop it, Jean. Leave me alone!"

The teacher walks over to Jean's desk and says, "Jean, you know that you are not to write on someone else's paper. I want you to turn around and do your work. That's a reminder."

The teacher writes Jean's name on his clipboard and continues to monitor her to redirect her back to work.

A few minutes later, Jean turns around and this time tries to grab Bert's paper. The teacher again approaches Jean. "Jean, you're obviously having a hard time doing your work without bothering your neighbors. Will you please take your work and go sit in the back of the class for the next five minutes? After class, I want you to fill out the behavior journal and think about what you should have been doing rather than bothering your neighbor."

The teacher puts a check by Jean's name.

Here's another example of the significance of being consistent:

An eighth grade math class was so disruptive, their teacher quit midway through the semester. When the new teacher arrived, she encountered constant disruptions as students talked back, shouted out, left their seats, and behaved belligerently.

On her first day, the new teacher explained her rules to the students. She told them what would happen when they followed the rules, and the corrective actions they would receive if they chose not to behave appropriately. The students in turn virtually ignored the rules. The teacher attempted to recognize those few students who were on task, but her comments fell on deaf ears.

She then began to give corrective actions from her discipline plan. Each time a student broke a classroom rule, she gave a corrective action. The students thought it was a joke and some tried to get as many checks as they could. By the end of the period that first day, nine students had reached the fourth step on the hierarchy, which meant that their parents were to be called. As she excused the students, the teacher clearly announced that she was going to be speaking to a number of parents that evening. One particularly belligerent young man responded, "No way any teacher is going to call all those parents!"

The next day in class the students compared notes and found out the teacher had meant what she had said. All the parents had been called. That same day four students reached the fourth level of the hierarchy. That night the teacher called their parents.

Over the next several weeks, the students periodically challenged the teacher. They soon realized that every time a student disrupted, there would be a corrective action. As the days went by, the students' respect for their new teacher grew. They began to place more value on her positive comments and recognition than on attracting her attention through disruptions. Her verbal support replaced the corrective actions. And learning replaced the chaos that had once existed in the classroom.

As this teacher said, "I never in my life had to be so firm and so consistent when dealing with my students." It was the students' behavior that told her she needed to set limits and to stick with those limits.

After correcting a student's behavior, recognize positive behavior at the first opportunity.

Here's a common problem many teachers share: After a student has been disruptive, after the student has received a corrective action, all the teacher does is focus on that student's negative behavior. The teacher is angry and is just looking for an opportunity to catch the student disrupting again.

Don't fall into this trap. Instead, take the first opportunity to recognize the student's appropriate behavior. You may have to provide another corrective action if the student continues to disrupt, but try to defuse the tension by finding something positive to say.

If you want to reduce your own stress and tension level, look for something positive the student is doing and acknowledge him for it.

Return to the example of Kirk and Stephen (see page 140). Each of the boys had received a check and therefore was to stay after class.

Kirk and Stephen are now working quietly, participating appropriately in their group. The teacher walks over to both of them.

Teacher: Kirk, Stephen, you both are working quietly, and you're both helping out the whole group. You are making much better choices about how to behave.

It should always be your goal to show students that you are more interested in focusing on their appropriate behavior. It will let them know that you want them to succeed and that you are there to encourage them, even if they have a few setbacks along the way.

Provide an "escape mechanism" for students who are upset and want to talk about what happened.

Many times after receiving a corrective action, students will want you to stop what you are doing and listen to their side of the story. Most of the time you will not be able to stop your lesson at that very moment. But you do want to let the students know that you care about what they have to say. In this situation, many teachers use an "escape mechanism" that allows students to defuse their anger and "get something off their chest" without disrupting the rest of the class. Escape mechanisms can include:

➤ Having the student write a note to you that you will discuss with him after class or when there is a break in the lesson

➤ Using a notebook to record misbehavior that allows space for students to write their comments

➤ Having students keep a daily journal or diary in which they can record any comments

If you use an escape mechanism, remember that it is not a substitute for talking with the student about improving her behavior. It is simply a tool that allows you to deal with a student's anger or frustration in a way that does not disrupt classroom instruction.

When a student continuously disrupts, "move in."

There may be times when a student will continue to disrupt even after being given a reminder or a corrective action. Too often, a teacher will get angry and continue to take one corrective action after another until the student is finally sent out of the classroom. This drastic reaction may not be in the student's best interest.

Here's an example:

Darcy, a sixth grade student, has just received a reminder and a check.

Darcy: Oh, c'mon, man. Just get off my case.

Teacher: *(Getting angry)* I'm sick of your attitude, Darcy. You say one more word and it's another check.

Darcy: I don't care. Give me another check.

Teacher: *(Getting angrier)* OK, now that's two checks. I'm not taking this from you, young lady.

Darcy: Give me another check. See if I care. Go on.

Teacher: Darcy, one more word and you're out of here.

Darcy: Word.

Teacher: That's it. Get out.

What happened here? This situation clearly got out of hand. How could you handle it more effectively?

Before you and the student both get angry, take control of the situation. Defuse the anger by talking one on one with the student.

Use the "moving in" technique.

Here's what to do:

➢ **Move close to the student.**

Walk over to the student. Get close. Show your concern. Tell the student quietly but firmly that her behavior is inappropriate.

➢ **Remind the student of the corrective actions she has received so far.**

Remind her what will happen next if the misbehavior continues.

The key to this technique is confidence and firmness in your behavior, your tone of voice, and your body language. You need to communicate to the student that you will not tolerate further disruptions because you care too much about her to let the situation escalate to a point at which the corrective actions imposed would keep her from participating in the class.

Look now at how Darcy could have been dealt with using the moving-in technique.

Darcy has just received a reminder and a corrective action.

Darcy: Oh, c'mon, man. Just get off my case.

The teacher walks over to Darcy's desk, leans down and makes eye contact, and speaks in a caring yet firm tone.

Teacher: Darcy, I'm concerned that your behavior is going to result in some corrective actions that you really don't want. You have been doing well in this class lately, and I would like to see that continue. You and I both know that you have been trying and succeeding in your work.

Now, you have received a reminder and a corrective action. One more inappropriate comment and you will stay behind two minutes after the other students leave. Do you understand?

Many times, physical proximity is all that is needed to help calm down a student and stop the disruptive behavior. Walk over to the student. Show your concern. Let the student know that the behavior is inappropriate. Let the student know that you want to help her stop herself. Let the student know that you care.

With older students, "move out."

With older students, it may be more appropriate to "move out" of the classroom to speak to the student. Removing the audience of peers may increase the effectiveness of your limit-setting efforts.

When you "move out," remember to:

➤ Stay calm.

➤ Avoid arguing with the student.

➤ Recognize the student's feelings.

When Students Challenge Your Authority

By providing corrective actions calmly and consistently, you will effectively help most students choose responsible behavior and stop most of the disruptive behavior in your classroom.

But in spite of these efforts, there are going to be some cases in which students will challenge your authority and confront you. These confrontations can take many different forms: anger, tears, and even tantrums. But whatever the form, all are designed to hook you emotionally, to push your buttons, and to escalate the situation so that you back down from the limits you have set.

Refocus an argumentative conversation.

When a student tries to manipulate you or argue with you, you must stay in charge and refocus the conversation. Do not get involved in an argument. Do not let the student pull you into a pointless exchange. Do not let a student push your buttons.

Instead:

➤ Stay calm.

➤ State what you want: "I want you to sit down and complete your assignment."

➤ Preface your "statement of want" with understanding for the student.

➤ Repeat your statement of want a maximum of three times. If the student still argues, let him know that he may be choosing to receive a corrective action.

For example:

Teacher: Tom, I want you to sit down and get to work on your assignment.

Tom: *(Visibly angry)* Why are you picking on me? Cynthia's not doing her work. She's just playing around, too.

Teacher: I understand, Tom, but I want you to sit down and start your work.

Tom: But why do I have to if Cynthia doesn't? It's not fair.

Teacher: Tom, I see you're upset, but sit down and begin your work.

Tom: But I see lots of kids who aren't doing anything.

Teacher: Tom, if you do not get to work immediately, you and I will call your father during recess. The choice is yours.

Please always bear in mind that this refocusing technique should be used only to defuse a student's anger. It should be used only when a student is trying to manipulate a situation in a way that is not in his best interest. Do not use this technique to cut off communication between you and the student. If the student has a valid argument, you need to accept his point.

For example, if a student begins to be disruptive because he's already completed the work you assigned, you may want to redirect his behavior. Begin by acknowledging his efforts. You may then want to assign additional work or to reward him with an activity he enjoys that will not disrupt the class.

Following are some disruptive situations and examples of how they can be handled both ineffectively and effectively.

Be firm in calming a student who cries or throws tantrums.

Sometimes young students become upset when given a corrective action. Many have learned that they can get their way by crying, and they will attempt to see if it works with you.

Teacher: Maria, I cannot allow you to push another student. Please go and sit by yourself in the time-out area.

Maria: *(Starting to cry)* I didn't mean to.

Teacher: Now, Maria, just relax. There's no need to cry every time I talk to you.

Maria: *(Sobbing harder)* But I didn't do anything. I only tapped her.

Teacher: Maria, just calm down. Please. I'm not angry with you. Calm down. You don't have to sit by yourself. Just blow your nose and settle down.

If a child's tears are out of character, obviously you need to focus on calming down the student and finding out what is going on. But for many children, tears are part of a pattern of behavior that enables them to manipulate adults to get their way.

Now see how a teacher could have dealt more effectively with Maria.

Teacher: Maria, I cannot allow you to push another student. Please go and sit by yourself in the time-out area.

Maria: *(Starting to cry)* I didn't do anything.

Teacher: Maria, I can see you are really upset. I can see you do not want to sit by yourself. But you chose to push Samantha, and therefore you have chosen to sit by yourself.

Maria:	*(Crying harder)* But I didn't do anything. I only tapped her.
Teacher:	Maria, I hear what you are saying. Now, please go sit in the time-out area. When you are calmer, I will call you back to the group.

The teacher was empathetic but firm. She listened to the student and showed that she understood her feelings. Yet she stood her ground. She let the student know that the corrective action stands, in spite of the tears.

Ignore covert anger and continue correcting the inappropriate behavior.

Middle and secondary students sometimes will attempt to hook you emotionally with their body language. Looks of defiance, slamming books, mumbling under their breath—such behaviors are meant to push your buttons. They often are successful and tend to trigger reactive responses from teachers.

Teacher:	Toni, I told you to cut it out. Stop playing with your makeup. Take out your book and get to work.

Toni slowly takes out her book while glaring at the teacher.

Teacher:	*(Showing anger)* What's your problem, Toni? Don't look at me like that, young lady.
Toni:	*(Rudely)* I'm not looking at you.
Teacher:	I'm tired of that attitude, young lady.
Toni:	Likewise.

This situation was going nowhere. The student hooked the teacher with a dirty look, and a confrontation ensued that neither could win.

Whenever possible, simply ignore the covert hostility of a student. By ignoring the behavior, you defuse the situation. Remember that what you really want is for the student to comply with your request. Whether or not the student does it in an angry manner is not the issue. The student is still complying with your expectations. Many students need the "angry way out" to save face.

Here's a better approach to the same situation:

Teacher: Toni, the direction was to do your work, not to put on makeup. Now please take out your book. That's a check.

Toni takes out her book while glaring at the teacher. Seeing that Toni is getting to work, the teacher calmly distances herself from her. Later, as Toni leaves the class, the teacher takes her aside and acknowledges her for getting to work.

By ignoring the angry look, the teacher defused the confrontation. It didn't get out of hand, and the student resumed her work.

In the face of overt anger, be calm yet firm.

Some students, especially those who want control, will provoke angry confrontations with a teacher to get their way. In dealing with such a student, it is critical that you remain calm and distance yourself from the anger of the student. Many teachers, however, allow themselves to get emotionally involved.

Here's an example:

Sheila is reading a magazine while she is in her learning group. The other students keep asking her to participate, but she angrily refuses and taunts them for doing their work.

Teacher: What's the problem?

Student: We need Sheila's help. She just keeps making fun of us and won't do anything.

Teacher: Sheila, what's going on? Is there something I can do to help you get started?

Sheila: These guys are all nerds. I'm not doing this stupid assignment.

Teacher: Sheila, watch your mouth!

Sheila: I can talk any way I want. I don't have to listen to you.

Teacher: (*Getting upset*) Yes you do. I am tired of you mouthing off at me.

Sheila: Well, I'm tired of you, too.

Teacher: You'll be sorry you ever said that, young lady.

Sheila: Yeah? What are you going to do? You're a joke. You are just a joke.

The teacher lost complete control of the situation by reacting emotionally. Nothing was accomplished. The disruption didn't stop; rather, it escalated. The student and teacher were upset and found themselves on opposite sides of the fence. It is safe to assume that future encounters between the two would be equally difficult, if not more so.

Following are a few guidelines for handling a student's overt anger more successfully.

First, use a paradoxical response. In this context, it means that the more upset the student becomes, the calmer you must become. The calmer you are, the more it will defuse the student's anger. Keep in mind that the student, when angry, may be accustomed to parents or teachers also becoming upset or angry. When the teacher stays calm, the student may not know how to react.

Next, move the student away from other students. Students who are angry want an audience. The audience feeds their emotions. Moving the student away can further defuse the situation.

Here's how the situation could have been handled:

Teacher: What's the problem?

Student: We need Sheila's help. She just keeps making fun of us and won't do anything.

Teacher: Sheila, what's going on? Can't you work with your group?

Sheila:	These guys are all nerds. I'm not doing this stupid assignment.
Teacher:	I can see you're upset, but I can't allow you to talk that way in class.
Sheila:	I can talk any way I want. I don't have to listen to you.
Teacher:	*(Calmly)* Sheila, please come outside with me. We need to discuss this. I cannot allow you to talk this way in class.
Sheila:	No!
Teacher:	Sheila, you have a choice. Either come outside with me or you will have to go to Mr. Boyer's office.
Sheila:	I don't care. Send me.
Teacher:	I'm sorry you made that choice. You need to go to the office now. I want to talk to you about this later so we can work this out.

While the situation could not be resolved immediately, the teacher remained calm and firm. The teacher communicated to the student that she cared about her and her choices in class, and that she was genuinely interested in improving their relationship. Even though the student may not comply immediately, the groundwork was laid for more positive encounters in the future.

Asking for Assistance

What do you do if the student refuses to leave? It does no good to argue with the student and keep telling her to leave. You will need to summon assistance.

You will need to have the backup of a discipline team. A discipline team is made up of administrators and/or other teachers or staff at the school. You need to contact the office when you have a problem you cannot deal with. The team comes to your classroom and assists you with the student.

In the scenario with Sheila, here's how the teacher could have successfully dealt with the situation if Sheila had refused to leave:

Sheila: I'm not leaving. I won't go.

Teacher: *(Staying calm)* Sheila, I cannot make you leave, but I will call the office and have someone escort you out.

Sheila: I don't care.

The teacher sends a student to the office with a note requesting assistance from the discipline team. A few minutes later, Mr. Boyer and two counselors walk into the classroom. The teacher briefly discusses the situation with them.

Teacher: I would like all students, except for Sheila, to please line up and come outside with me.

After the students have left the classroom, the administrator walks up to Sheila.

Mr. Boyer: Sheila, we recognize that you're upset and that you do not want to leave the classroom. You do not have a choice in this matter. You must leave the classroom with us now.

The discipline team escorts Sheila from the classroom.

A discipline support team is critical in dealing with such serious situations. Unless you know you have the support of administrators when dealing with highly difficult students, it is unlikely that you will have the confidence to set the limits students need to manage their behavior.

Using Your Own Judgment

You have learned that consistency in your use of corrective actions is key to the success of your discipline plan. Students must know that misbehavior carries with it a corrective action—every single time.

In most cases, this guideline is absolutely correct. In reality, however, there will be times when your professional judgment tells you that it is not in a student's best interest to use a corrective action. Trust your judgment.

Consider these situations:

Situation #1

There is a student in your class who is usually well behaved, attentive, and responsive. One day, for no apparent reason, his behavior is highly disruptive. Because this behavior is so clearly out of character, it is much more appropriate for you to sit down and talk to this student, to try to find out what's wrong rather than issue a corrective action.

All your educational and disciplinary measures should be guided by your genuine concern for your students' well-being. Therefore, an obviously troubled student may benefit more from your empathy and understanding than from your corrective actions. All the student may need is a sympathetic ear to be able to cooperate again.

Situation #2

A student in your class has a serious problem controlling her temper. You may feel justifiably that providing a corrective action at a certain moment might provoke an outburst of anger that could prove hard to handle or disruptive to the entire class. It might be more appropriate to deal with the behavior at lunch, at recess, or after class. Since your goal as an educator is to assist your students in choosing appropriate behavior, the best course of action in some situations may be to avoid a situation altogether that could make a student erupt in anger.

Situation #3

One of your students is extremely upset and is crying. Providing a corrective action when a student is disturbed in this way would be meaningless. Until the student has calmed down, there's no point in sending her to time-out or having her write in the behavior journal. Corrective actions are meant to help your students manage their own behavior. If a student is too upset to fully appreciate why she receives a corrective action and how to improve her behavior, nothing will be accomplished. Therefore, wait until the student has calmed down.

The point is this: Don't just blindly follow your discipline hierarchy. It is meant to guide you, not to control you. In all situations, you must use your professional judgment to determine which responses are in the best interest of your students. All situations do not merit a black-and-white response. Pay attention to the gray areas. Know your students and use that knowledge to guide your disciplinary responses.

Your goal is to establish a positive and caring relationship with all students. If you're unsure how to respond, ask yourself, *How would I want my own child to be treated in this situation?*

Let your answer to that question guide you.

REMEMBER...

➤ Be consistent. Corrective actions must be provided each time a student chooses to disrupt.

➤ Give corrective actions in a firm yet calm manner. The positive effects of corrective actions are undermined if you show hostility or anger.

➤ Refocus students who attempt to argue with you.

➤ After a student receives a corrective action, take the first opportunity to recognize something positive the student is doing.

➤ Provide an "escape mechanism" for students who are upset and want to talk about what happened.

➤ "Move in" when a student is being continually disruptive.

➤ With older students, use the "move out" technique when students continually disrupt.

➤ Stay calm if students challenge your authority.

➤ When your professional judgment tells you that it is not in a student's best interest to provide a corrective action, trust your judgment. Your disciplinary hierarchy is a guide, not unquestionable law.

Chapter 13

Pulling It All Together:
Integrating Behavior Management and Teaching

The previous chapters addressed teaching behavioral expectations, giving supportive feedback, redirecting nondisruptive off-task behavior, and firmly and consistently using corrective actions when disruptive behavior arises.

How can you put it all together? How can you integrate all of these techniques into your teaching routine?

The art of teaching is the ability to blend academics and behavior management efforts into a cohesive whole. In this chapter, you will learn how to integrate these behavior management skills throughout the school day—while you are working with students and while you are teaching academics. Through the examples given, you will see that successful classroom management conducted by a skilled teacher is almost invisible. It is woven so well into the fabric of her teaching style that an observer might not even be aware a strategy is at work.

You will look at examples of three classroom situations at three different grade levels: K–3, 4–6, and 7–12. Whatever the grade level you teach, read each of these examples. All contain points that will be useful to you.

In each of these situations, you will observe how teachers can instruct their students, consistently deliver supportive feedback, redirect off-task behavior, motivate students to stay involved, and use corrective actions to stop disruptive behavior. As you read, think about how you can integrate these skills into your own classroom.

Implementing Behavior Management Skills During a Transition

The first example focuses on a primary classroom during a transition period.

The scene: A second grade classroom. It is the first week of the school year.

The teacher picks up a bell and rings it. The students have learned that this signal means they are to stop, look, and listen.

Teacher: José has stopped reading.

Sean has his eyes on me.

Corrine is not talking.

Good! You all remembered what to do when I ring the bell.

It's time to get ready for recess. When I say go, I want you to stand up, put your chairs under your desks, and line up by group at the door. Let's quickly review how you need to line up.

Tom and Juanita, can you show us all how to put our chairs under our desks and how to walk quickly and quietly to the door?

The two students model following these directions.

Teacher: Juanita, Tom, you have a great memory for following directions. That's exactly right!

Now, when I say go, group one will put their chairs under their desks and quickly and quietly line up.

Then I will ask the other groups to go in order. Wait your turn. Wait until I tell your group to go.

All right, group one. Ready, go.

The students in group one begin to follow the direction.

Teacher: Max, Vivian, and Cynthia all remembered to push their chairs under their desks. They walked quickly and quietly to the door.

The teacher writes Max's, Vivian's, and Cynthia's names on the board under a heading marked "Classroom Superstars." The three students beam with pride.

After writing these names, she walks over to the door, positioning herself close to where the students are lining up. She scans the room, monitoring the students as they make the transition.

Teacher: All right, group two . . . ready, go.

Anna, Rico, and Lindsay are putting their chairs away and are moving quickly and quietly.

Two students from group one, Cora and Jennifer, start acting silly in line. The teacher moves next to them and puts her hand on Cora's shoulder.

She speaks quietly to the two girls.

Teacher: Cora and Jennifer, what are you supposed to be doing?

Cora: Lining up at the door.

Teacher: That's right. Let's line up quietly then, OK?

Jennifer: OK.

Teacher: Group three . . . ready, go.

As group three begins to line up, one student, Karl, picks up a ball from the equipment bin and throws it across the room. The teacher quietly retrieves the ball and walks over to Karl. She speaks calmly to him.

Teacher: Karl, we do not throw balls in the classroom. That's a reminder.

She writes Karl's name on her clipboard and then returns her attention to the class.

Teacher: Cora and Jennifer, nice job waiting in line. Group four . . . ready, go.

After the last group has lined up, the teacher speaks to the class.

Teacher: I have a great group of listeners here. Most of you remembered to line up at the door quickly and quietly, with your hands to yourself.

Now look more closely at what happened during this transition.

On the surface, the teacher gave the students a direction, and the students followed that direction. But more significantly, underlying this teacher's initial direction was the fact that she didn't drop her behavior management efforts for a second.

Recognizing that it was the beginning of the year, she took the time to teach the directions she wanted the students to follow, then took additional time to have students role-play those directions. She didn't assume her students would know or remember how to line up appropriately.

This teacher clearly understands that transitions can provide ample opportunity for disruption. Unless students know exactly what they are expected to do, and unless the transition is carefully monitored, a teacher can suddenly find herself with 30 students running from one activity to another.

To prevent further problems, the teacher not only taught her directions, she also used liberal amounts of positive support to reinforce students who were following those directions. Her use of behavioral narration and writing names on the "Superstars" section of the board let her students know that she noticed their positive behavior.

Because monitoring behavior is key to managing behavior, she positioned herself in a location where she would best be able to keep tabs on most students during the transition. Therefore, when two students did go off task, she was able to gently redirect them back to more appropriate behavior, without raising her voice and without disrupting the class. Likewise, when another student disrupted, she wasted no time giving him a firm reminder.

By using effective classroom behavior management techniques and integrating them with sound teaching techniques, this teacher led her class smoothly through a beginning-of-the-year transition.

Implementing Behavior Management Skills During a Small-Group/Cooperative-Learning Situation

This example depicts a sixth grade class as they move into cooperative-learning teams.

The scene: A sixth grade classroom. The students are about to begin a cooperative-learning assignment.

Teacher: Today in your learning teams, I want your groups to come up with the answers to the problems that are written on the board. Before you get started, though, let's quickly review the directions when you're in learning teams.

The directions I expect you to follow are:

1. Move quickly and quietly to your team.

2. When in your team, discuss only the assignment.

3. All members participate.

4. If you need help, raise your hand.

Any questions? OK? Ready, go.

The students quickly and quietly arrange their chairs into their groups. The teacher monitors the students as they assemble.

Teacher: Ladies and gentlemen, that was quick and that was quiet! And that's a point for the class toward radio time on Friday.

As the students begin to work in their teams, the teacher circulates from group to group, checking to see that everyone understands the assignment and is able to get started. As he moves from group to group, he takes a moment to offer a quick, encouraging moment of recognition to each.

Teacher: That's it, group four. Looks like you're tackling those problems! Group five, nice job dividing up parts of the problem among the team.

He sits down for a moment with one group that is having trouble understanding the assignment. As he is sitting with the group, he periodically looks up and scans the other groups. As he scans, he notices that students in group three aren't settling down to work.

He directs a purposeful "look" at these students, a look that lets everyone in the group know he's aware that they are off task and that he expects them to get to work. When the students begin to work, he returns his attention to the group he's sitting with.

Teacher: OK. You're making a good start. Now, let's just review for a moment how you can break down this problem.

A few minutes later, the students in group three stop working and begin shooting rubber bands at the group next to them. The teacher walks over to the group. He speaks to the students calmly and firmly.

Teacher: Karen, Monica, Kevin, and Emil. The directions were to work quietly with your team to come up with answers to the problems on the board. There is no shooting of rubber bands allowed in class. You all have a reminder.

As he writes their names on his clipboard, the students begin protesting loudly.

Karen: Hey, we're just having fun. It's no big deal.

The teacher makes firm eye contact with Karen. His very look lets Karen know that in his classroom it is, in fact, a big deal. When he speaks, it is with firmness.

Teacher: I expect all of you to get back to work. If I have to talk to any of you again, it will be after class.

Monica and Emil begin to get to work. Kevin and Karen, however, are still acting up.

Kevin: Why are you so hard on us?

Karen: Yeah, give us a break. You're worse than my parents.

Teacher: Kevin, Karen, you have chosen to stay after class. We will discuss this then. I expect you to get to work immediately. If this doesn't happen, you will choose to have your parents called. Now, I'm going to sit down with you and make sure you get to work.

The teacher sits with group three. They settle down and get to work on their assignment.

Teacher: Kevin, what are you supposed to be doing? Can you review what the assignment is for all of us?

After group three has settled down to work, the teacher continues to circulate among the other groups. After a few minutes, he walks back over to group three, bends down, and speaks.

Teacher: OK. Now you're all doing a great job. I know that group three can work together as well as any other group in this room. Good work.

Small-group situations provide students an opportunity to work together, learn to cooperate, and share responsibility. Often, though, the disruptive behavior of one or more group members can take a group off task and limit the academic value for all. As demonstrated in this example, a successful teacher must consistently monitor learning groups and provide support, redirection, and corrective actions if necessary.

To prevent problems proactively from rising, the teacher in this example began by reviewing the specific directions students were expected to follow during a cooperative-learning session. He made sure, even before the students moved into their groups, that his expectations were made clear to everyone.

Once the students were dismissed into groups, he immediately implemented a classwide reward system, recognizing the students with a point toward a goal, in this case radio time. He began circulating from group to group immediately, offering encouraging words and a smile as students began to get to work.

When he noticed that one group was off task, he quickly redirected them with a look that let them know they had better get to work. A few minutes later, when the off-task behavior continued, he walked over. They had already been given an opportunity to change their behavior. Now he was ready to follow through with the first step on the discipline hierarchy: a reminder.

After receiving a reminder, two students challenged him verbally. The teacher did not engage them in conversation. He did not get angry. He did not plead with them to "shape up." Instead, he followed through with his discipline hierarchy and provided a corrective action, telling the students that they could discuss it later, after class. He did not cut off communication but offered them a later opportunity to voice their disagreements.

Once the corrective action was given, the teacher sat down with these students to redirect them back to their assignment. As he continued monitoring their behavior, they eventually settled down and got to work, and the teacher gave the students positive feedback.

The result? All students in this class were able to succeed at this lesson. Despite the disruptions, this teacher's skilled use of behavior management techniques allowed him to move past the problems and enjoy a successful teaching experience.

Implementing Behavior Management Skills During a Class Discussion

In the final example, follow a ninth grade teacher as she conducts a lecture and class discussion.

The scene: A ninth grade classroom. The students have recently returned from winter vacation and are a bit restless as the teacher conducts a discussion in a history class.

Teacher: We're going to continue our discussion today about the Underground Railroad. But before we get started, let's quickly review the directions we follow during a class discussion. Who can give me one direction?

Students raise hands.

Teacher: Francesca? *(The teacher repeats the directions as students give them.)* Eyes on the person speaking. Good. Tamara? That's right, raise your hand if you want to speak. OK, George, what's another direction? Notebooks and pencils out, everything else away.

Great. During our discussion I will be looking for everyone to follow these directions. Remember that we're still working on earning points for a pizza party. When I see everyone following directions, I will add a point to the chart.

OK, let's get settled and ready to begin.

The students put their books away and, one by one, sit upright and pay attention.

Teacher: Bill and Ken have their desks cleared of everything except notebook and pencil, and they are ready.

Tamara has her notebook out. Rebecca's ready, too. It looks like we're all set. That's a point for the class.

The teacher adds a point to her chart.

Teacher: We were talking yesterday about the Underground Railroad...

As she speaks, the teacher immediately begins circulating among the students. While she moves around the room, she makes a point of looking directly at different students. She keeps them aware of her with a smile, a nod, or a look. She uses her presence and her gestures to keep the students' attention.

Teacher: We have learned that the men and women who led the slaves out from the South on the Underground Railroad were called conductors...

While speaking, she notices that one student, Rodney, is looking out the window and not paying attention. Without missing a beat, she makes her way over to Rodney's desk and stands by him.

Teacher: Let's talk now about how the Underground Railroad functioned. Rodney, let's say you're a conductor on the Underground Railroad. Sue and Melissa, you're slaves who want to escape to the North. Rodney doesn't know you; he has never met either of you. How do you think the three of you could plan the journey? Rodney certainly can't just go over to visit Melissa and Sue, can he? Can he pick up a phone and call them? Can he send a telegram to them? How do you think an Underground Railroad conductor made arrangements with the slaves he would take north?

Think about this question. I'm going to ask one of you to answer, but I'm going to expect all of you to comment on that answer.

She waits a few moments for all students to consider the question.

Teacher: OK. Who can tell us how Rodney, the conductor, would make contact with Melissa and Sue, slaves who want to run away to the North?

The teacher waits a moment as more and more students raise their hands.

Teacher: Jason?

Jason answers.

Teacher: That's a good thought. Class, what do you think? I would like to see thumbs up for those of you who agree with Jason. *(The teacher pauses.)*

Now thumbs down if you don't agree.

Thumbs sideways if you just don't know.

Chris, you had thumbs down. Why don't you agree with Jason's answer?

The discussion continues in this manner as the teacher involves all students in questions and answers.

Teacher: Good work, everyone, on participating. That's another point for the class. Rodney, Melissa, and Sue, thanks for letting us use you as examples on our Underground Railroad journey.

Now I would like all of you to please open your notebooks and copy down the three questions that are written on the board. Write an answer to each one. No talking while you're working.

When you're finished, take out your book and begin reading Chapter 4. The assignment is on the board. Any questions?

The teacher scans the room, moving over to Rodney. She leans down and quietly speaks to him.

Teacher: Rodney, good work getting started on the questions. You're doing great today.

Most of the students get on task. Nathan, however, isn't paying attention. Sitting next to him are two students, Rachel and Gary, who are on task. The teacher walks over to these students and quietly leans in to speak to them.

Teacher: Rachel, Gary, nice job getting right to work.

As the class begins writing, Sandy and Leo, who are seated at the back of the room, begin talking loudly to each other. The teacher walks over to them and speaks to them in a quiet voice.

Teacher: Sandy and Leo, the rule is no shouting out in this classroom. That's a reminder for both of you. The direction was to copy down the questions on the board and write your answers. Please get to work.

A few moments later, Sandy starts teasing Leo. They begin laughing and causing disruption. The teacher quickly approaches again.

Teacher: Sandy, Leo, this is the second time I have had to speak to you. Both of you will be staying after class to fill out a behavior journal.

Were you aware of everything that went on during this lesson? This teacher made it possible for every one of her students to start off on the right track, stay involved, and learn. She was not burdened by disruption because she has worked preventive and proactive techniques into her teaching style. She kept all her students attentive, responsive, and alert throughout her discussion. She never let students go off task, nor did she ignore a disturbance once it presented itself. At the same time, her lesson never had to stop for a moment.

She orchestrated a successful lesson, beginning with a review of the specific directions. She then acknowledged the students who were following those directions by using a classwide support system.

Take special note of the teaching techniques she used, which allowed her to integrate behavior management so smoothly.

➤ She redirected an off-task student by drawing him into the discussion, giving him a "part" to play.

➤ She kept eye contact with students as she spoke, keeping them involved and attentive.

➤ When she asked questions, she involved the entire class, giving plenty of time for all students to consider the question.

➤ She added some humor to her lecture.

➤ She invited full-class participation through a "thumbs-up" technique.

And through it all, she gave consistent supportive feedback.

When disruptive behavior did arise, this teacher dealt with it firmly. No arguments. She didn't interrupt the flow of her teaching and thus didn't take any time away from her students' learning.

Was she overbearing? Did she stifle her students with negativity?

No. This teacher demonstrates an artful balance between positive support and limit setting.

Positive Outcomes

As the teachers in these three examples illustrate, classroom behavior management isn't something you learn, then put aside "in case you need it." Behavior management skills must be integrated into all of your interactions with students on a daily basis.

Your body language—a genuine smile, a gesture, a look—the caring tone of voice as you speak, and a supportive comment at the right moment are vitally important efforts you make to redirect behavior. The consistency and concern with which you handle disruptive behavior is another key element for the success of your discipline plan. In combination, these are the skills that make the difference between a productive, involved class and a classroom mired in problems.

Once you become accustomed to using behavior management skills to deal proactively with student behavior, you will find that many disruptions will never arise. You will also find that those that do arise can be dealt with successfully. Above all, you will find that you will have more productive, cooperative, and positive relationships with your students.

REMEMBER...

➤ The art of teaching is the ability of teachers to blend academics and behavior management efforts into a cohesive whole.

➤ Skilled classroom management is almost invisible, woven into a teaching unit without distracting from the subject matter.

➤ Skilled classroom management balances positive support and limit setting every single teaching day.

➤ Behavior management must be integrated into all your interactions with your students.

DIFFICULT STUDENTS

Consistent use of the classroom management skills presented in the previous sections will enable most educators to teach 90 to 95 percent of their students to choose responsible behavior.

The remaining 5 to 10 percent—the difficult students you sometimes encounter—are the focus of this section. You know who these students are. They are the ones who may ignore your rules, may not respond to your corrective actions, and may disrupt the entire class. They are the students who argue with you, chronically disturb other students, and view your classroom as a place in which to perform their own antics rather than do their work.

Besides interfering with the normal flow of classroom work, these are often the students who push your buttons and make you forget about being calm and assertive. More than anyone else, however, difficult students need your unwavering determination to help them behave appropriately. The strategies offered in this section are meant to help you meet these needs.

Chapter 14—Responding to Difficult Students

Chapter 14 looks at the way in which teachers respond to students who present behavioral challenges.

Chapter 15—Building Positive Relationships

Chapter 15 discusses the importance of looking beyond the behavior of your challenging students and getting to know them as individuals.

Chapter 16—Developing an Individualized Behavior Plan

Chapter 16 presents strategies for customizing a discipline plan that is geared to the specific needs of your students.

Chapter 17—Getting Support from Parents and Administrators

Chapter 17 discusses approaches for involving parents and administrators in your efforts to support your most challenging students.

Chapter 14

Responding to Difficult Students

You have done everything suggested in this book. You have created a discipline plan that clearly communicates to your students what you expect of them and what they can expect of you in return when they meet your expectations and when they don't. You have diligently taught and retaught your classroom rules and your system of supportive feedback and corrective actions. You have implemented your plan with great care and consistency. You have used a proactive approach.

Generally, your students are responsive. They follow your rules most of the time. On the few occasions that they don't, all you ever need are redirection techniques and a reminder here and there to make sure they cooperate. Most of your students relish receiving your positive comments and your rewards, and they share your pride when they succeed at following the rules. In other words, your classroom runs pretty smoothly—except . . .

There are a few students who don't seem to respond to any of the disciplinary measures you have employed so far. They go through your discipline hierarchy on a regular basis, yet their behavior shows only temporary improvement. They are only temporarily motivated by your supportive feedback. But if you do not continually acknowledge them or stand near them most of the day, they fall right back into their old patterns. They continue not paying attention, they continue disrupting your teaching routine, and they continue disturbing other students. You are at the end of your rope. These students are draining your energy. You are ready to explode. You are ready to give up.

As difficult as the situation may seem, it's important not to turn away from these students. There are solutions.

Your first step in working with difficult students is to examine your overall attitude and how you respond to these students in class.

A Progression of Ineffective Responses

Even the most proactive teachers—those equipped with a discipline plan—often find themselves ineffective when challenged by difficult students. They begin to complain about a student's behavior rather than act to change it. They begin to blame the student or themselves, and they stop using the discipline plan rather than search for individual solutions.

It is not uncommon for teachers to go through a progression of reactive responses, ranging from underreacting to overreacting.

Having discarded the discipline plan and deeming it ineffective, teachers tend to underreact or become passive with difficult students. They may respond by begging and pleading with the students or ignoring their behavior altogether. The hope is that with enough warnings or by letting nature take its course, students will decide to change their behavior on their own.

Let's look at two situations, as examples of how teachers underreact.

Situation # 1: Begging and pleading with students

A third grade teacher directs her class to line up for recess. Three of the boys, who are usually disruptive during such transitions, immediately leap from their desks and race to the door, pushing and shoving each other to be first in line.

The teacher pleads with them from across the classroom. "Boys, how many times do I have to ask you to walk in the classroom? I'm tired of having to repeat myself. Won't you please see if you can walk properly? Next time will you please try and remember to act like third graders?"

Situation #2: Ignoring inappropriate behavior

A seventh grade teacher is giving a lecture in front of the class. As he speaks, he notices that two of his students at the back of the room are talking to each other. They are not paying attention to what he is saying, and they are disturbing the students around them. The teacher simply ignores the students and continues his lecture. He thinks to himself, "There's nothing I can do about these students anyway."

After many fruitless attempts to keep these students on task, both teachers become frustrated. Their discipline plans, containing the skills and techniques for dealing with disruptions and confrontations, have been discarded. Begging and pleading doesn't work. Ignoring the inappropriate behavior doesn't work. The teachers feel completely powerless and do not know what to do next. They communicate this to their students in every interaction with them.

Passive responses often lead to threats and anger.

When a teacher feels powerless and does not take action, the situation will eventually deteriorate because the student's misbehavior will most likely continue. Given enough time, the teacher's frustration will build up to a point where it turns into overt anger. In such situations, teachers tend to overreact. They may berate their students or threaten them with idle promises. Here is an example:

Situation #3: Using the threat of consequences

In a sixth grade class, there is a belligerent student who is provoking other students around her. The teacher tells her to stop bothering her classmates and get to work. The student responds, "I don't want to do any of this stupid work."

The teacher throws up his hands and says to the student, "What's wrong with you? The same thing happens with you every day! I keep warning you that you had better shape up or you will be in big trouble. If you don't get to work this minute, you're going to the principal's office." The student giggles and continues her disruptive behavior. Clearly frustrated, the teacher just walks away. As the student expects, the teacher gives no corrective action at all.

Because past warnings were not effective, this teacher escalated his response, hoping that the threat of a severe consequence would help the student choose to self-correct her behavior. However, empty threats of punishment rarely help a student. The problem will undoubtedly continue, leading to more frustration on the teacher's part. In the end, the teacher usually gets angry and sends the student out of the classroom. Returning to situation #3, let's look at an example of this type of overreactive response.

Situation #3, continued: Becoming hostile

After being threatened with being sent to the office, the student giggles and continues her disruptive behavior. By now the entire class is off task. The teacher sees no hope of gaining control of the situation. His adrenaline is pumping. He gets more upset with the student.

The teacher steps over to her and shouts directly at her: "That's it. You've got a lousy attitude and I've had it with you. One more word out of you and you're out of this class."

"That's fine with me," she snaps back. The teacher opens the door and gestures her out of the classroom. The student storms out of the room, slamming the door behind her. In spite of her earlier bravado, her humiliation is obvious.

This kind of angry confrontation escalates the situation. Nobody wins, and the teacher and student are more alienated than ever before.

In each of the above situations, the teachers' responses were certainly understandable, but they were not what the students needed. Begging students, ignoring their behavior, or threatening them with consequences did not stop the disruptive behavior and did not result in the ultimate goal: having the student return to productive work.

Practical Solutions

Difficult students are difficult precisely because they have no history of compliance with rules. They have not learned how to respect rules, and they have little or no experience in participating in a cooperative community. If you want your classroom to be a cooperative community, each and every member needs to learn, understand, and adhere to the rules by which it operates.

This means that you cannot give up on a particularly trying student and discard your discipline plan and the behavior management techniques that go with it. Instead, to manage your difficult students, you need to find an individualized approach that falls within the framework of your general classroom discipline plan.

How can you accomplish giving this added attention without focusing all your energy on just these few difficult students? First and foremost, as obvious as it may sound, you must recognize and accept that you are having difficulties with a particular student or group of students. Admitting that there is a problem will allow you to analyze it openly and clearly. You will be able to recognize your feelings of frustration, and you will be able to recognize the responses that are generated by that frustration.

Only if you recognize that you respond to difficult students in an ineffective manner will you be able to return to the effective responses discussed throughout this book. Then you will be prepared to take the additional steps necessary to change the student's behavior for the better.

In the following chapters, we will provide suggestions for helping students with chronic behavior problems become more successful. First, we will discuss the importance of reaching out to your students to build open, trusting, and caring relationships. Then we will discuss how to individualize the management of a student's behavior, focusing on one-on-one conferences and behavior plans that address specific behavior goals. Finally, we will suggest strategies for involving your administrator and the student's parents in supporting your efforts.

Remember, if your classroom discipline plan doesn't work with your difficult students, it is not your fault. And it is not the fault of your discipline plan. You may simply have to go above and beyond your general discipline plan and behavior management techniques to reach out to your students. With difficult students, it is crucial that a limit-setting structure is balanced with a supportive and caring relationship.

Note: The ideas in the following chapters are based on concepts drawn from Lee Canter's *Succeeding With Difficult Students* (1993), published by Solution Tree (formerly National Educational Service). For a more in-depth study of working with difficult students, please refer to that book.

REMEMBER...

➤ About 5 to 10 percent of your students can be considered difficult because they have not responded to your discipline plan.

➤ Difficult students tend to push your buttons and cause you to react emotionally.

➤ Some teachers tend to ignore difficult students because of negative expectations of their ability to help these students in the past.

➤ Some teachers, out of frustration, tend to beg and plead with their students, hoping they will self-correct their disruptive behavior.

➤ Some teachers, out of frustration, tend to threaten difficult students with severe consequences.

➤ The key to working with difficult students is to develop an individualized approach based on each student's unique needs.

Chapter 15

Building Positive
Relationships

When dealing with difficult students, you must go beyond the
guidelines of your classroom discipline plan. You must go beyond relying on the behavior management techniques that are effective
with most of your students.

Your difficult students' negative attitude toward you is not meant to be
taken personally. Usually their actions stem from their distrust of adults in
general and teachers in particular. Experience has taught them that adults
cannot be counted on. They believe that teachers are not on their side.
They assume you do not care about them. They expect hostility and dis-
respect from you, just as you expect it from them.

Offering Personal Support

One key factor alone can change such a student's outlook. This key factor
is the presence of a supportive adult who is willing and able to provide
positive guidance in the child's life. You can be this adult.

Look beyond the behavior and see the student.

Difficult students need an adult who is able to distinguish between a
student's misbehavior and a student's value as a person. If you want to
be effective in reaching difficult students, you need to show that you

care about and value a student as a unique individual even though he may have behavior problems. You need to be able to look beyond the behavior and see the child. This is the first step in building a foundation for trust.

Build trusting relationships.

Difficult students will not reach out to you. But they might change their attitude and behavior if you reach out to them. With difficult students, you must go beyond praising students and supporting them when they meet your expectations. You must also use special approaches that enable you to reach out and consistently build positive and trusting relationships with them on an individual basis—supportive relationships that show you really do care about your students. Those are the relationships that raise a student's self-esteem.

Establishing relationships with students does not mean that you become their friend. You need to maintain a professional distance. But keeping your distance does not mean keeping your relationship within the academic realm. It means becoming actively interested in your students as people: in their lives, their relationships, their friends, and their hobbies. Relating to a student on this level will increase his sense of worth as a human being and as a student. You communicate the message that he matters. You demonstrate that you care.

Ways to Demonstrate Interest

Given the time constraints you face as a teacher, how do you establish and cultivate a unique, caring relationship with your students, including, most importantly, your difficult students?

You do not need to have a weekly heart-to-heart with every one of your students. There are simpler strategies that will show your students you notice them. There are subtle ways of incorporating openness, accessibility, and caring into all your interactions with your students.

Here are some suggestions to start your own collection of positive techniques:

➤ Greet your students by name as they enter your classroom.

➤ Stop to chat with them in the hallway, in the cafeteria, at recess, before class.

➤ Make a point of initiating conversations.

➤ Monitor and modify your tone and body language to convey openness and friendly concern.

➤ Show your interest and give complete attention when your students are talking to you.

➤ Express care, concern, and empathy.

➤ Smile and show a sense of humor.

➤ Take a student interest inventory at the beginning of the year to learn about your students' favorite activities.

➤ Bring up nonacademic topics of mutual interest.

➤ Share appropriate personal interests and experiences.

➤ Call a student after a bad day to discuss how you might have a better day tomorrow.

➤ Call a student after a good day and compliment her on her success.

➤ Send get-well notes, or call home if a student is sick.

➤ Write positive notes to the student and his parents.

➤ Attend school activities: plays, dances, athletic events. Don't forget to mention a student's accomplishments the next day as you greet her at the door.

➤ Recognize and offer supportive feedback for a student's strengths and achievements, both academic and nonacademic.

➤ Help others to see the student's positive side. Write positive notes to parents. Mention a student's achievement to one of his other teachers. Help a student if he is in trouble with the school's administration.

We'll take a closer look at just a few of these techniques.

Take a student interest inventory.

Establishing a personal relationship with students means knowing something about them personally. Be prepared. At the start of the year, take time to find out who your students are. Learn their likes and dislikes, their favorite activities, their hobbies and interests. You will find that these insights will help you get to know your students better. And the better you know your students, the more you will be able to reach out to them as individuals.

On the facing page is a sample student interest inventory. Make this inventory the first homework assignment of the year. For younger kids, conduct the inventory orally with the help of a parent volunteer or a classroom aide.

Greet students at the door.

Here's one of the best opportunities you have each day to show students you care. When they come into class, plan to be there at the door, greet them, and find something special to say to each of them. This is an especially effective way to make personal contact with those students who need your individual attention and caring words.

Here's how one high school science teacher used this technique:

"Every day, before the start of each period, I'm at the door. My kids probably think it's where I like to hang out, but I have a different reason for being there. As each student passes into my room, I greet them. And as I greet them, I find something to say—something positive, something personal, something friendly:

'Good job on your test yesterday, Tonya!'

'Glad to see you back, Mark. Hope you're feeling better.'

'Tran, how are you today? Great jacket!'

Student Interest Inventory

Name:

Adults who live with me:

Name: Relationship:

Name: Relationship:

Name: Relationship:

Brothers and sisters:

Name: Age:

Name: Age:

Name: Age:

Best friends:

What I like to do most at home:

My favorite school activities:

My favorite after-school activities:

My favorite TV show:

My favorite book:

My favorite movie:

If I had one wish, I would want to:

When I grow up, I would like to:

School would be better if:

If I had a million dollars, I would:

What my teacher(s) did last year that I liked the most:

What my teachers(s) did last year that I liked the least:

"To put it another way, every day I start my class with each student having received some sort of individualized attention, whether it's a smile, a joke, or a statement of concern.

"This isn't an accident. I make sure I'm at that door. I have it planned. I know what I'm doing and it works. I care for these kids. I know we may have some rough times once class starts, but I want every one of them to know that each day is a new day, so let's start with a fresh and optimistic attitude! And for those kids who especially need some thoughtful words from me, it's a great opportunity to say something positive without singling them out in class."

Spend a few special minutes with a student.

Sometimes the most precious and valuable gift you can give your students is your own time. Spending recess or lunch with a student can make all the difference in the world to a student who needs a caring, guiding hand.

As one teacher summed it up:

"Some kids are just needier than others. Some kids just demand more attention. Many of these kids come from homes where no one takes the time or effort to show they care. I realize that I have a responsibility to give them the special attention they need. So I give it. This is the only way I can be sure that I'm addressing their need for a caring person in their lives, and doing everything I can to help them succeed."

Make a phone call after a difficult day.

Here's a powerful positive technique to use after you have had a difficult day with a student. Students are accustomed to hearing repercussions from teachers when there has been a problem. Turn the tables and bridge the communication gap by reaching out to let the student know you care.

Here's what such a phone call might sound like:

Teacher: Stanley, this is Mr. Jones. I'm calling because I feel bad about the difficult day you and I had. I don't like it when you and I have problems in class, and I could see that it wasn't easy for you, either.

Stanley: No, it wasn't.

Teacher: Why were you so upset?

Stanley: I don't know.

Teacher: Is there anything I can do to help?

Stanley: Well, not really. I mean, sometimes the work is a little hard for me. That's all.

Teacher: What do you mean?

Stanley: Well, it's just hard.

Teacher: The next time you feel the work is too hard, let me know and we will work together. I could sit with you for a few minutes and go over the assignment. How does that sound?

Stanley: Well, all right.

Teacher: Stanley, I know you can be successful in my class, and I really want to help you. We don't have to have more days like we did today. Tomorrow we're going to start all over. No hard feelings. We will work to make things better. How does that sound?

Stanley: Yeah, all right. I'll see.

Teacher: OK. I will see you tomorrow. And don't forget that if you're having any problems, you can come to me.

By modeling a positive, caring attitude, you invite the same. Your students will recognize that you too are a human being with a life outside the classroom. When this happens, a bond is established. You offer your loyalty, and they in turn will offer theirs.

Rewards and Results

Building positive relationships does not require that you go out of your way on a daily basis. The situations that will require you to spend time on the phone or in a private conversation with a student are most likely few and far between. Small gestures will work wonders. Listen attentively, take your students' thoughts seriously, smile at their accomplishments, offer a sympathetic ear when problems arise, say please and thank you, and above all, show your respect. These simple efforts will pay off, and you may find very quickly that your difficult students aren't so difficult after all.

REMEMBER...

➤ Show your students that you care about them as unique individuals, despite their problematic behavior.

➤ Make it your goal to establish positive relationships with even the most difficult students.

➤ Begin by working subtle ways of presenting yourself as an open, accessible, and caring person into all your interactions with your students.

➤ Learn more about your students. Have each of your students fill out a student interest inventory at the beginning of the year.

➤ Use the student inventory throughout the year by addressing what you have learned when the opportunity presents itself.

➤ Give one-on-one attention by sharing your own time with students at recess or lunch, or before or after class.

➤ Attend school activities to see your students perform.

➤ Make positive phone calls.

➤ Call students at home after a particularly difficult day. Let the student know you care and that you will work with her to improve conditions at school.

Chapter 16

Developing an Individualized Behavior Plan

B y itself, establishing positive relationships with your difficult students is not guaranteed to turn around their behavior. As with any student, the balance between offering support and setting limits is important. It may even be more important for difficult students.

While most of your students respond to the general structure you set with your discipline plan, your difficult students need something more—more time and attention. And these students often need something different—different disciplinary measures and supportive strategies. In other words, you need to adapt your behavior management techniques to suit these particular students.

One-on-One Conferences

There is no better way to begin individualized behavior management than with a serious yet sensitive one-on-one conference with a student about her problematic behavior.

A one-on-one conference is a meeting between you and a student to discuss and try to solve a specific behavior problem. Your goal in this conference is not to punish, but to listen to the student and give caring and firm guidance.

A one-on-one problem-solving conference should be brief. You should not have to meet for more than a few minutes. The conference must be conducted at a time when you can give the student your undivided attention. No other students should be around to interrupt or overhear what you are discussing.

Keep in mind that the purpose of this conference is to help the student choose more appropriate behavior. Even if you are interested in finding out why she misbehaves, and even if you want to help this student with the situation that is potentially responsible for her behavior problems, remember that you are not counseling the student or taking on the role of psychologist. You are her teacher, and you want to help her succeed in your classroom. The first step is to help her behave in a way that will allow her and everyone else to learn. This must be the focus of your conference.

Following are some basic concepts to keep in mind when you meet with a student for a one-on-one conference.

Show empathy and concern.

Your goal is for the student to understand that her behavior stands in the way of her success in your classroom. Ultimately, you want her to choose more responsible behavior because she understands that only by doing so will she succeed. Let the student know you are concerned about her behavior because her actions are not in her best interest. Let the student know you care about her, even though her behavior is problematic. Let the student know you are not meeting to punish her but to help her.

> "I can see you had a hard time controlling your anger in class today. I'm concerned about this because I know how difficult it is for you to get along with the students sitting near you when you are so angry. And I also know you don't like it when I send you to time-out. Let's take some time now to talk about this."

> "You and I had a really rough day. I'm concerned about that. I can see that you were really angry with me and that you feel I'm picking on you. Let's see if we can make this situation better."

Question the student to find out why there is a problem.

Behavior is never just behavior. There usually is a reason for a student's problem. In fact, there may be a variety of reasons, so don't count out anything. The student may be inattentive because she can't see the board from where she's sitting. Or the student may be a discipline problem because her parents are about to get a divorce. Be sensitive and caring when you try to find out what's bothering the student.

> *"Did something happen today to get you so upset?"*

> *"Are other students bothering you?"*

> *"Do you have trouble seeing the board?"*

> *"Do you have trouble understanding what you read when you read quietly to yourself? Do you need to read things out loud to understand them?"*

> *"Are there any problems at home that I can help you with?"*

Determine what you can do to help.

What can you, as a caring teacher, do to help the student solve the problem? You may discover a simple answer that will get the student back on track.
For example:

➤ If a student is having trouble in class with another student, move his seat.

➤ If a disruptive student is seated at the back of the class, consider moving her forward. Proximity to you will allow you to monitor her more closely, and it will enable her to concentrate more easily.

➤ Contact the parents if you feel the student needs additional help and support from home.

➤ Boost your supportive feedback toward the student, not just your corrective actions. Look for the first praiseworthy behavior after the conference. Then send home a positive note or a behavior award.

> Can you adapt the classroom situation to accommodate the student's learning style? For example, if a student has trouble working independently, allow her to work with a partner as often as possible.

> A student may need academic help that you, a tutor, or a peer study buddy may be able to provide. Make that help available.

> Speak with the school counselor. Make sure the student knows that such help is available at the school.

Discuss these or some of your own suggestions with the student.

Determine how the student can improve his behavior.

Part of your conference needs to focus on how the student can behave differently in the future.

"I understand you're having trouble with the other boys, but you cannot fight in this classroom. Let's talk about other ways you could deal with these situations instead. What do you think you could do rather than fight?"

Some students may not be willing or able to share their own ideas and feelings about more appropriate behavior. Don't react angrily or irritably to their inability to respond. Help them by pointing out ways to behave more appropriately.

Agree on a course of action.

Combine your ideas with the student's ideas and agree on what both of you can do to improve the situation.

"I know it's hard to keep from getting angry with other kids sometimes. I think your suggestion about just walking away is a good one. I'm going to help, too. Every day that you don't get into a fight, I'm going to send home a note to your parents."

State that you expect the student to change his behavior.

Clearly state your expectations for behavior in the future.

> *"I'm going to work with you to solve this problem. You're a good student and you're smart. I know you can behave responsibly. But remember that fighting is not allowed in class. Anytime you fight, you will be choosing to go to the principal."*

If an initial one-on-one problem-solving conference does not significantly improve a student's behavior, use a second one-on-one conference to discuss an individualized discipline plan with the student.

Individualized Discipline Plans

An individualized behavior plan is designed to adapt the concepts of your regular classroom discipline plan to meet the unique needs of a particular student. An individualized behavior plan can help teach the student to behave responsibly. Furthermore, it can provide the basis for developing the cooperative relationship with that particular student which so far seems out of reach.

Once again, balance structure and caring.

An individualized discipline plan will include:

➤ **The specific behaviors expected of the student**
Select one or two behaviors at a time to work on. Choose those that you believe are most important to the student's success.

➤ **Meaningful corrective actions to be imposed if the student does not choose to engage in the appropriate behavior**
Difficult students often do not respond to the basic corrective actions used in your discipline hierarchy. Often you will find that the student reaches the same corrective action on the hierarchy each day.

For example, each day a student might reach the third step on the hierarchy and stay after class for two minutes. It would appear that the student really does not mind staying after class and thus the corrective action is not effective.

It is important to note, however, that this student always stops short of the corrective action that involves calling the parent. The teacher can conclude that it may be effective to individualize this student's discipline plan so that the first time she disrupts, instead of a reminder, instead of staying after class, her parents are immediately contacted.

It may also be appropriate with some difficult students to provide corrective actions that are not on your classroom discipline hierarchy. It may be necessary, for example, to keep a student in at recess or lunch. Or, you may want the student to come after school for detention.

> **Meaningful positive recognition to be given when the student does behave appropriately**
Your supportive feedback, as always, should begin with verbal recognition. Once you have implemented an individualized behavior plan, look for every opportunity to recognize the student's appropriate behavior.

Back up your supportive feedback with other forms of positive recognition that you feel would be appropriate. Would a positive note home to the parents be appreciated? Would the student enjoy a special privilege, such as being appointed class monitor?

Perhaps the student would benefit from and enjoy some personal attention from you. Would it be appropriate to have lunch with the student? Or does the student just need to talk with you for a few uninterrupted minutes?

No matter what corrective actions and what positive recognition you choose, it is absolutely critical that you balance corrective actions with supportive feedback when dealing with difficult students.

Present the individualized behavior plan to the student.

Meet with the student in a one-on-one conference. Be firm yet empathetic and caring. Let the student know that you are on her side. Assure the student that you are there to help, not to punish. Let her know that you established this personalized discipline plan because you cannot allow her to engage in behavior that is not in her best interest. Make sure she realizes that you want her to succeed and that you have confidence that she will.

Gear the discussion to make sure it is age-appropriate for the student. Follow the guidelines outlined below.

Grades K–3

Young students are very concrete. Your discussion must be very specific about how the student should behave, what will happen when she does not, and what will happen when she does. You may want to role-play the behaviors you want the student to engage in.

Grades 4–6

At this age, students do not want to be told what to do. They want to feel they have a say in how they choose to behave. Whenever possible, involve the student in discussing how she should change her behavior, and how you will correct inappropriate behavior and reward appropriate behavior.

Grades 7–12

Most students this age do not want lectures from adults. Any problem-solving session with these students should be conducted in as matter-of-fact a manner as possible. Listen to the student and invite participation.

For many students, talking about behavior problems is very touchy. It's all mixed up with self-image and self-esteem. Give your support. Listen attentively. Take her thoughts seriously. Approach the student with firm but caring resolution. Above all, make sure you end all one-on-one conferences on a positive note. Express your confidence that the student will be able to manage her behavior successfully.

Be consistent.

Individualized behavior plans will work only if you implement them consistently and continually. This has two very important implications.

First, it is paramount that you use the corrective actions you decided on each and every time the student disrupts. Should the student comply with your rules for a day or two, don't stop using the corrective action when she disrupts on the third day because "she's been so good." Whenever the student disrupts, the corrective action has to follow, no matter how good she's been up to that point.

Second, as much as you must correct each and every disruption, you must reward each and every improvement in behavior. Make sure you let the student know that you appreciate the extra effort it takes to manage her behavior. Reward her generously with the supportive feedback you chose. Offer verbal recognition, send home a note, or have lunch with her.

Pledging Commitment and Effort

Don't compare the students who have chronic behavior problems to the other students in your class. Not everyone is the same, nor should they be. Don't expect and reward only perfection. The road to successful behavior management is long and arduous, particularly with some students. You will probably experience a few setbacks. Succeeding with difficult students takes perseverance and patience.

Above all, it takes a willingness to consistently communicate to the student that you care and that you are not going to give up. You will be there for the ups and you will be there for the downs. You are prepared to do whatever is needed to help the student succeed.

This is a message that many students have never heard before. When a difficult student realizes that a caring adult has made such a commitment, it will leave a lifelong impression. The student in turn may commit to improve his behavior and thus improve his chances for success in school and, ultimately, in life.

REMEMBER...

➤ A one-on-one problem-solving conference is a meeting between teacher and student to discuss a specific problem.

➤ The goal of a problem-solving conference is for the student to gain insight into her behavior and ultimately to choose more responsible behavior.

➤ A problem-solving conference should include the following steps:

1. Show empathy and concern.

2. Question the student to find out why there is a problem.

3. Determine what you can do to help.

4. Determine how the student can improve her behavior.

5. Agree on a course of action.

➤ If your initial problem-solving conference doesn't bring the desired results, use a second one-on-one conference to discuss an individualized behavior plan.

➤ An individualized behavior plan

1. should include only one or two of the student's most critical problem behaviors.

2. must establish firmer, more meaningful corrective actions that will motivate the difficult student to respond.

(continued)

REMEMBER... *(continued)*

3. should be balanced with increased supportive feedback.

4. will work only if the teacher consistently provides the firm corrective actions in the case of misbehavior and the positive rewards for behavioral improvement.

➤ Keep in mind that with difficult students, the balance of structure and care is particularly important.

➤ Don't expect corrected behavior immediately. Value and reward improvement.

Chapter 17

Getting Support From Parents and Administrators

Parents and administrators can each offer unique support that will often have a powerful impact on students, particularly on difficult students with whom little else seems to work.

It is frequently difficult, however, for teachers to ask for this assistance. As discussed in Chapter 1, the foundation of this difficulty lies in the "myth of the good teacher." According to this myth, a good teacher should be able to handle all behavior problems on his own and within the confines of the classroom. If a teacher is competent, he should never need to go to the principal or to a student's parents for assistance.

This myth places a burden of guilt on teachers, especially those who must deal with difficult students. These feelings of inadequacy tend to keep teachers from asking for the help they need.

As we have pointed out, this myth is nonsense. No one teacher, no matter how skilled she is or how much experience or training she has had, is capable of working successfully with each and every student without support.

This chapter will focus on how you can get the support you need. But before you ask for assistance from parents and administrators, you must make sure you are equipped to get that help when you need it.

First Steps to Obtaining Support

So that you are fully prepared to solicit help, be sure you have done all you can on your own to solve the problem. Be proactive by taking these measures:

➤ Share your classroom discipline plan with parents and your administrator.

➤ When a problem arises, take steps to deal with it on your own before asking for help.

➤ Document a student's behavior and the steps you have taken to handle it.

Let's take a closer look at each of these points.

Share your classroom discipline plan with parents and your administrator.

Parents can't support your behavioral expectations if they don't know what those expectations are. If parents are to become partners in their children's education, they must be well informed about your discipline plan. After all, contacting parents is an important part of your discipline hierarchy. If you want them to be involved when you need them, parents need to know why you have a plan and what your rationale is for the rules, the positive support, and the corrective actions.

At the start of the school year, give students a copy of your discipline plan to take home to their parents. Include a letter that explains why a classroom discipline plan is important. Ask parents to discuss the plan with their children, sign the plan, and send a signature portion back to you.

On the following page is a sample discipline plan letter to parents.

If you want the support of your administrator, she should be fully aware of exactly how you plan to deal with student behavior and under what circumstances you will send a student to her office. Before you implement your discipline plan, you must present it to your administrator. Explain your goals for teaching students responsible behavior and explain your rules, supportive feedback, and corrective actions.

You and your administrator must work together. The administrator is your ace in the hole for working with difficult situations.

Dear Parent,

I am delighted that _____ is in my class this year. With your encouragement, your child will be a part of many exciting and rewarding experiences this academic year.

Since lifelong success depends in part on learning to make responsible choices, I have developed a classroom discipline plan that affords every student guidance in making good decisions about their behavior and thus an opportunity to learn in a positive, nurturing classroom environment. Your child deserves the most positive educational climate possible for growth, and I know that together we will make a difference in this process. Below is an outline of our classroom discipline plan.

Rules: 1.   Follow directions.

2.   Keep hands, feet, and objects to yourself.

3.   No swearing or teasing.

To encourage students to follow these classroom rules, I will recognize and support appropriate behavior, as well as send "good news" notes home and make positive phone calls home. However, if a student chooses to break a rule, the following steps will be taken:

First time a student breaks a rule:	Reminder
Second time:	5 minutes working away from group
Third time:	10 minutes working away from group
Fourth time:	Call parents
Fifth time:	Send to principal

Be assured that my goal is to work with you to ensure the success of your child this year. Please read this classroom discipline plan with your child, then sign and return the form below.

Sincerely,

- -

I have read the discipline plan and have discussed it with my child.

Parent/Guardian Signature _____ Date _____

Comments: _____

_____

When a problem arises, take steps to deal with it on your own before asking for help.

Whenever appropriate, you should attempt to handle a student's disruptive behavior on your own before you speak to the parents or administrator about the situation. Both will want to know what actions you have taken to help the student. Assure them that you have attempted to solve the problem on your own first.

Remember, your goal is to teach the student to make good behavioral choices. If you involve parents or the administrator too soon, you are not allowing the student the opportunity to change his own behavior.

Document a student's behavior and the steps you have taken to handle it.

Early in the school year, your experience and intuition will guide you in recognizing those students who may have problems as time goes on. It is vital that you begin documenting problem situations right away. Having complete anecdotal records is imperative when seeking the support of administrators and parents.

An anecdotal record should include the following information:

➤ Student's name and class

➤ Date, time, and place of incident

➤ Description of the problem

➤ Actions taken by the teacher. For example:

Name:	*Bryan Shelby*
Date:	*3/16/01 Time: 10:45 Place: Yard*
Problem:	*During recess Bryan shoved Mike Collins while Mike was waiting in line to play handball. Mike fell to the ground.*
Actions taken:	*Bryan was counseled and then benched during lunch recess.*

Getting Support From Parents When a Problem Arises

There are several specific steps effective teachers take to get the support they need from parents when students exhibit behavior problems in the classroom.

Contact parents at the first sign of a problem.

A common complaint among parents is that teachers wait too long before contacting them about a problem. It doesn't matter whether the problem occurs the first week of school or even the first day. As soon as you become aware of a behavioral problem that parents should know about, contact them.

How do you know when you should contact a parent about a problem? Many situations are very clear: severe fighting, extreme emotional distress, a student who refuses to work or turn in homework. Don't think twice about involving parents when these situations occur.

But what about the day-to-day instances that may not be so obvious? Often you must use your own judgment.

If you are uncertain about contacting a parent, use the "your own child" test. This test will put you in the position of the parent and help clarify whether parental help is called for.

Follow these steps:

1. Assume you have a child of your own the same age as the student in question.

2. If your child was having the same problem in school as that student has, would you want to be called?

3. If the answer is yes, call the parent. If the answer is no, do not call the parent.

For example, if your child did not turn in one homework assignment, would you want to be called? Probably not. If your child did not turn in homework for three days in a row, however, you most likely would want to know. The "your own child" test helps you treat parents the way you would want to be treated and also serves to focus your attention on problems that need parental involvement.

By using this test, you will increase your contacts with parents. This increases the probability of getting parental support when you need it.

Plan what you will say before you speak to a parent.

Before you pick up the phone or meet with the parents, you need to outline what you are going to say. These notes will help you think through and clarify the points you want to make. Having the notes in front of you while you're speaking will help you communicate more effectively.

Here are the points you will want to cover:

1. **Begin with a statement of concern.**
   Because a conference or call can be stressful and upsetting to parents, it is important that you begin the conversation by showing your concern for the student rather than by just bluntly stating the problem.

   "Mr. Johnson, I care about Mark and I feel that his behavior on the yard is not in his best interest."

2. **Describe the specific problem and present pertinent documentation.**
   Explain in specific, observable terms what the student did. If you are meeting face-to-face, show the parent your records that document the student's behavior.

   "This week Mark was involved in four fights. You can see here that he was sent to the office by yard aides twice on Wednesday and again on Thursday and Friday."

3. **Describe what you have done.**
   Explain how you have dealt with the problem and what effect your actions have had on the student.

   "I have spoken with Mark about his behavior, and he has been given detention each time he's been involved in a fight. His behavior has remained the same."

4. **Get parental input on the problem.**

   Listen carefully to what the parent has to say. Here are some questions you may want to ask:

   > *"Has your child had similar problems in the past?" (It may be useful to examine school records to determine if the student did have problems previously and if the parent was aware of them.)*

   > *"Why do you feel your child is having these problems at school?"*

   > *"Is there something (divorce, separation, siblings, a move) going on at home that could be affecting your child's behavior?"*

5. **Get parental input on how to solve the problem.**

   Parents usually know their child better than anyone else does. They may have a good idea that could help solve a specific problem. Ask the parent:

   > *"What do you feel I can do to help your child?"*

   > *"How do you feel we can work together to help your child solve this problem?"*

6. **Tell the parent what you will do to help solve the problem.**

   You have already explained what you have previously done and what effect your actions have had. Now, let the parent know exactly what you are going to do.

   > *"Mr. Johnson, since this problem has continued, I am going to change corrective actions for Mark. From now on, each time he fights on the yard, he will be sent immediately to the principal and you will be called. He won't receive any warnings first, and he won't be sent to detention."*

7. **Explain what you need the parent to do to solve the problem.**

   Just as carefully, you must explain what you would like the parent to do to help solve the problem.

   > *"Mr. Johnson, we need to work together to help Mark improve his behavior here at school. His fights on the yard are completely*

unacceptable. It's hurting him. It's not in his best interest. Anytime you are called about a fight, I would like you to follow through at home with your own disciplinary measures."

8. **Let the parent know you are confident that the problem can be worked out.**

   Well-chosen words will punctuate your message with assurance.

   "Mr. Johnson, I am confident that if we work together we can make this a better year for Mark. I've dealt with many children who have had this problem, and I can assure you that we will be able to turn things around if we are united in our efforts."

9. **Tell the parent that there will be follow-up contact from you.**

   A parent needs to know that you are going to stay involved. Provide this reassurance by giving a specific date for a follow-up call or note.

   "Mr. Johnson, I am going to call you next Thursday evening to let you know how things are working out for Mark."

10. **Recap the conference.**

   To avoid confusion and assure that your message was clear, you may need to clarify all agreements. You can do this by restating and writing down what you are going to do and what the parent is going to do. Keep this information in your files.

   Teacher: We have agreed to a number of things today. Here's what I have agreed to do: I am going to change the corrective actions for Mark. From now on, each time he fights on the yard, he will be sent immediately to the principal and you will be called. No more warnings. No more detention.

   Now, I want to be sure I am clear about the steps you're going to take. What is it that you are going to do?

Parent: Anytime that I'm called about Mark's fighting, I'll take away privileges from him at home. And I'll do it every time, not just whenever I feel like it.

Teacher: I think this is going to make a big difference, Mr. Johnson. Thank you for working this out with me. Now Mark will know that we're working together to solve this problem.

Establish a positive relationship with all parents.

Most parents report that they hear from teachers only when there is a problem. Imagine how much easier it would be to contact a parent about a problem if you had already established a positive relationship. Instead of calling a stranger with bad news, you would be calling a parent with whom you had already exchanged good news, shared information, and had other positive communication.

Establishing positive communication with all parents should be one of your priorities. It's as simple as writing a welcome note at the start of the year, making a phone call to relate something positive about a student, or taking the time to send home a note applauding a student's effort.

Getting Support from Your Administrator

When it comes to dealing with disruptive students, an administrator can offer a teacher support that is uniquely effective.

Here are some ways an administrator can help you help your students:

➤ Reward positive behavior.

➤ Counsel with the parent or student.

➤ Institute in-school suspension.

➤ Request that parents of disruptive students come to the school.

Let's take a closer look at each of these points.

Reward positive behavior.

Many teachers view an administrator's role in dealing with problem students as that of the "bad guy." This is a shortsighted view. We have seen phenomenal results occur when the principal serves as a positive motivator who recognizes appropriate behavior.

A first grade teacher tells this story:

"The principal at my school is really the foundation of my positive recognition program with difficult kids. In this school, there is no one individual whose positive attention carries more weight or importance than the lady who sits in the big chair in the office."

This teacher rarely sent students to the principal's office when there was a problem. She sent students to the office when they improved their behavior. She said:

"I'll never forget one little guy who had so much trouble controlling his anger. He really worked hard and eventually learned to use words rather than his fists. I was so pleased that I told him he needed to make a superstar visit to the principal. At first he was afraid. Because of his experiences at his old school, he couldn't imagine a visit to the principal being fun. But he went, and he came back with a big smile on his face. A few of the principal's well-chosen words and a big hug were the best motivators ever for this student."

Counsel with the parent or student.

Have you ever had difficulty convincing a parent to come in and talk to you about a problem a student is having? A phone call from an administrator can provide the added encouragement an otherwise reluctant parent needs. Likewise, having your principal sit in on a conference can demonstrate to parents how concerned the school is about their child's success and can be the key in motivating a parent to take action in helping to solve a particular problem.

The same can be said for having the principal spend a few minutes speaking with a student about her behavior. The weight of the administrator's position can carry the clout necessary to let some students know that they need to choose more appropriate behavior at school.

Institute in-school suspension.

Some students' behavior is so disruptive that the administrator must remove them from the classroom. An in-school suspension room is an alternative disciplinary action to placing students on out-of-school suspension. (This option is particularly valuable in situations in which students prefer unsupervised suspension at home to being in school.)

Here are some guidelines for instituting an effective in-school suspension room:

➤ The room must be well ventilated and well lighted.

➤ The room must be monitored at all times by an administrator, teacher, aide, or other responsible adult.

➤ Students sent to in-school suspension must do academic work in silence. If the student disrupts the room, he will earn extra hours there.

➤ The student stays in the room for a few hours, up to a maximum of one day for older students.

➤ Parents should always be notified when a student receives in-school suspension.

➤ If there is no in-school suspension room available and the office is too distracting to students, teachers might support one another with the buddy system. Two teachers agree to provide one another, as needed, with a desk at which a student will do assigned work during in-school suspension.

Note: It is very important that in-school suspension be held only in appropriate areas. Locations such as bookrooms and closets are never to be used as in-school suspension areas.

In-school suspension can prove to be one of the best support services an administrator can offer a teacher in dealing with highly disruptive students who need help in controlling their behavior.

Request that parents of disruptive students come to the school.

Some students are so defiant and disruptive that extra effort needs to be taken to help them control their behavior. With middle and secondary students, it can be helpful to have the principal request that the parent come to school and spend the day—all day—in every class with the child.

This can be a powerful action that motivates many disruptive students to choose more appropriate behavior. The parent can see exactly how the child behaves in school. More importantly, the student feels pressure from his peers about the parent being at school. Typically, one visit by the parent is all that is necessary to motivate most students to choose to behave, as illustrated by the following:

James was an extremely defiant student. He repeatedly sent the message to his teachers that "I'll do what I want, when I want." Individualized behavior plans, parent conferences, and in-school suspension all proved futile.

As a last resort, the principal met with James and his mother and made it clear just how concerned he was about James's behavior. He told the mother that if James disrupted one more time, he would ask her to come to school to monitor James's behavior in class, all day long. James was appalled at the idea. "No way is she coming to school!" he said.

The principal emphasized that it was James's choice whether she came or not. If he disrupted again, she would be asked to come. Reluctantly, the mother agreed.

For the next few days, James behaved appropriately. Then he tested the limits to see what would happen. As promised, the administrator called James's mother, and the next day she came to school. James sulked from class to class, his mother close by. As he later said, "That was the worst thing that ever happened to me."

James made sure it never happened again. He chose to behave in a more positive manner that enabled him to be more successful in school.

REMEMBER...

➤ Parents and administrators can offer the kind of support that you need and to which difficult students respond.

➤ It is a myth that you should be able to handle all behavior problems on your own.

➤ You must take proactive measures in order to secure the support you need for working with difficult students.

1. Share the classroom discipline plan with parents and the administrator at the beginning of the year.

   a. Send a detailed letter explaining the plan to parents, with a signature portion to be returned to you.

   b. Meet with your administrator to explain your discipline plan and the circumstances under which the administrator will be involved.

2. When a problem arises, take steps to deal with it on your own first.

   a. Don't involve parents or the administrator prematurely. Allow the student time to change her behavior.

3. Factual, complete documentation of a student's behavior must be compiled, including any steps you have taken to handle the problem behaviors. Anecdotal records should include:

   a. Student's name and class

   b. Date, time, and place of incident

(continued)

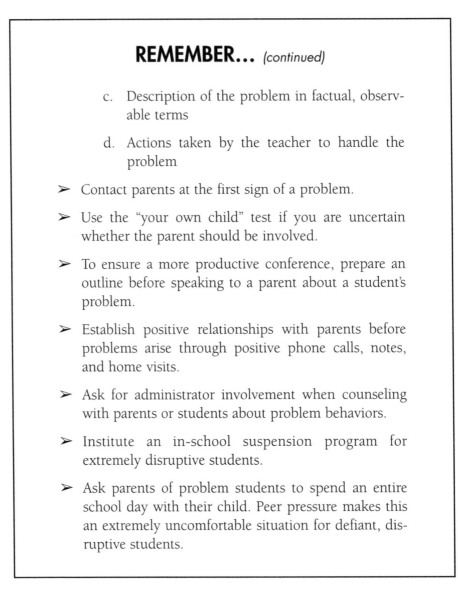

REMEMBER... *(continued)*

    c. Description of the problem in factual, observable terms

    d. Actions taken by the teacher to handle the problem

➤ Contact parents at the first sign of a problem.

➤ Use the "your own child" test if you are uncertain whether the parent should be involved.

➤ To ensure a more productive conference, prepare an outline before speaking to a parent about a student's problem.

➤ Establish positive relationships with parents before problems arise through positive phone calls, notes, and home visits.

➤ Ask for administrator involvement when counseling with parents or students about problem behaviors.

➤ Institute an in-school suspension program for extremely disruptive students.

➤ Ask parents of problem students to spend an entire school day with their child. Peer pressure makes this an extremely uncomfortable situation for defiant, disruptive students.

Conclusion

Going Beyond

It has been the goal of this book to provide you with a solid foundation to establish a classroom in which you can teach and your students can learn—a classroom that addresses the individual needs of each student and your individuality as a teacher. To this end, the concepts presented here are part of an ongoing process, not the final word.

Adapting Assertive Discipline

Teachers who are most effective in dealing with student behavior, in raising student self-esteem, and in increasing students' potential for academic success often go beyond the concepts presented in this book. They take the Assertive Discipline skills and techniques they have learned with them into their classrooms, then adapt them to their own personal teaching style and to the unique needs of their students.

Involve students in the process.

Some teachers do not determine the rules for their classroom by themselves. Instead, they involve students in the decision-making process and periodically ask the entire class to evaluate the rules to see how effective they are.

Many teachers involve students in teaching one another the classroom rules or the specific directions. In some cases, teachers assign one or two students to be behavior monitors. When new students are enrolled in the classroom, they are taught the rules by the behavior monitors rather than by the teacher.

Other teachers hold class meetings when they feel they are providing too many corrective actions. At these meetings, they ask the students to give feedback on how problem situations might be handled more appropriately.

Other Ways to Help

Your students deserve the best you can give them. For some students, that means seeking answers from a variety of resources.

Some teachers incorporate other classroom management theories and approaches into their Assertive Discipline efforts. This is perfectly acceptable. It is the professional responsibility of any educator to analyze, synthesize, critique, and adapt the various behavior management theories available. It is only through this process that your own teaching style will evolve and your ability and confidence to handle the many classroom challenges will increase. The flexibility that is built into Assertive Discipline, however, allows teachers to effectively meet the needs of all types of students.

Many behavior problems can be eliminated by changing instructional strategies. For example, teachers who have difficulty managing student behavior when lecturing in front of the class often report that they experience fewer discipline problems when students work and study together in cooperative-learning groups.

It is often difficult to keep today's generation of computer-savvy, television-watching students attentive, interested, and motivated in class. For many students, the immediate response of the computer and the quick cuts and vibrant visuals on television make the classroom a comparatively lackluster place to be. By learning to create a more relevant and stimulating curriculum, teachers can cut down on student boredom and the resulting disruptive behavior.

Behavior problems in class are frequently the result of conflict between students. Teachers often report that conflict resolution programs, designed to give students skills to resolve conflicts among themselves, have had a positive impact on reducing behavior problems in the classroom.

Effort, Caring, and a Hopeful Future

When all is said and done, providing the optimum classroom environment for your students does not end when you close this book. Your continual efforts are needed to ensure that your classroom is an active learning environment. When the time comes to alter or change an approach, you need the skills to do so and the confidence to proceed.

Above all, never forget the power and impact you can have with children. A quotation from Haim Ginott's *Teacher and Child* says it best.

> *"I have come to a frightening conclusion. I am the decisive element in the classroom. It is my personal approach that creates the climate. It is my daily mood that makes the weather. As a teacher I possess tremendous power to make a child's life miserable or joyous. I can be a tool of torture or an instrument of inspiration. I can humiliate or humor, hurt or heal. In all situations it is my response that decides whether a crisis will be escalated or de-escalated, and a child humanized or dehumanized."*

And finally, we leave you with one last thought—a concept that underscores the power of the teacher and the responsibility that goes with it. Remembering it is sure to motivate your efforts each and every day.

Children are our hope for the future. But we are the hope for theirs.

Appendix

The following references support the concepts and strategies upon which Assertive Discipline is based.

1st Edition, 1976

The vast majority of children are capable of behaving appropriately. When adults believe that children can behave, clearly state the behaviors they expect from children, and are prepared to back up their words with actions, there is a high probability that children will behave appropriately. However, when adults do not believe that children are capable of behaving, their communication is often vague and unclear. Children can determine by an adult's words and tone whether or not the adult believes they can behave (Foster, 1971; Lesoff, 1975).

Assertiveness training teaches that individuals can learn how to more effectively express their wants and needs to others (Smith, 1975). A classroom teacher has wants and needs in the classroom that must be expressed to the students in a manner that does not abuse the rights of the students.

Behavior modification strategies are useful in managing student behavior. A key to motivating students to behave appropriately is to provide positive consequences for appropriate behavior and negative consequences for inappropriate behavior (O'Leary, et al., 1973).

2nd Edition, 1992 and 3rd Edition, 2001

Educators sometimes think of classroom management as classroom discipline. Yet as much as 80 percent of classroom management relates to problem prevention as opposed to intervention. Spending time early in the year to set high standards for behavior will result in better behavior throughout the year (Frieberg, 1996).

Teachers who demonstrate high levels of success in motivating difficult students to choose appropriate prosocial behavior can best be described as *proactive*. The approach to behavior management most likely to succeed is a preventive one, where the teacher thinks about, anticipates, and plans for potential problems before they occur (Doyle, 1980).

Teachers who are unsuccessful with difficult students are often labeled *reactive* (Paine, 1983). By reactive, it is meant that the teacher is unprepared and tends to respond to misbehavior in a highly emotional manner. Teachers who are effective in handling student behavior react in a confident, assertive manner (Jones, 1987; Smith 1975). In addition, teachers who have positive expectations of their ability to handle students are more successful. Positive expectations are the foundation of effective classroom management (Rosenthal & Jacobson, 1968).

Student behavior in academic achievement is strongly influenced by the quality of the teacher-student relationship. Students who feel that their teachers like them have a higher frequency of positive classroom behavior than those who do not (Rosenshine, 1983; Davidson & Lang, 1960).

Classrooms do not function effectively without guidelines for student behavior. Many students do not come to school with a basic understanding of how to handle materials, how to work individually, and how to work cooperatively in groups. Rules and procedures help them understand appropriate behavior (Evertson, Emmer, & Worsham, 1999).

Students need to know teachers' expectations. Creating a carefully planned system of rules and procedures makes it easier to communicate those expectations. A set of procedures gives students explicit directions in how the rules translate to various classroom activities. An effective preventive approach is to teach students the specific directions they are expected to follow in all classroom activities. A significant amount of class time at the beginning of the school year should be devoted to teaching students specific directions (Evertson, Emmer, & Worsham, 1999; Paine, 1983). Mixed messages and vague directions leave many students wondering how to comply with a teacher's requests. Clean rules help students understand and follow guidelines until they become second nature (Coloroso, 1997). In addition to rules and procedures, there should be goals for students. Goals are aspirations to be accomplished over a long period of time (Evertson & Harris, 1997).

Consistent use of positive reinforcement is a highly effective means of motivating students to behave in an appropriate manner. Effective teachers utilize a high-frequency level of verbal recognition and other back-up reinforcers. Reinforcement strategies have been demonstrated as being effective with both individual students and the entire class (Paine, 1983).

No matter how effective teachers are at establishing positive relationships with students—teaching prosocial skills, and providing consistent encouragement and reinforcement of appropriate behavior—teachers will at times need to provide negative consequences to stop the disruptive behavior (Paine, 1983).

Various authors have presented concepts designed to help direct non-disruptive off-task students back on task (Evertson, Emmer, & Worsham, 1999; Long & Newman, 1980). Such strategies prove effective in motivating students to increase the frequency of their productive on-task behavior (Jenson, Sloane, & Young, 1988).

When it is necessary to use consequences for disruptive behavior, they should be provided in a calm, matter-of-fact manner, with eye contact and, when possible, in close proximity to the student (Van Houten, et al., 1982). In addition, a key factor in the effectiveness of consequences, particularly with difficult students, is the consistency with which the consequences are provided. When difficult students engage in disruptive behavior, they need to be provided the consequence on a regular basis. Inconsistent use of consequences will prove to be ineffective (Morgan & Jenson, 1988).

Many students with emotional or behavioral problems require individualized behavior plans. The general classroom plan will not be sufficient to motivate such students (Lovitt, 1973; Jenson, Sloane, & Young, 1988). When working with difficult students, administrator back-up may be needed. An administrator can provide back-up to a classroom teacher by first intervening with students when there is severe disruptive behavior. In addition, support can be provided by establishing resources, such as an in-school suspension room, detention room, or discipline squad (Jones, 1987; Englander, 1989).

Recommended Reading
and Bibliography

Albert, L. (1991). *Cooperative discipline.* Circle Pines, MN: American Guidance Service.

Brookover, W. B., et al. (1996). *Creating effective schools: An in-service program for enhancing school learning climate and achievement.* Holmes Beach, FL: Learning Publications.

Canter, L., & Canter, M. (1993). *Succeeding with difficult students: New strategies for reaching your most challenging students.* Bloomington, IN: Solution Tree (formerly National educational service).

Charles, C. M., et al. (1999). *Building classroom discipline.* New York: Longman.

Coloroso, B. (1997). Discipline that makes the grade: Could your school's program pass inspection? *Learning, 25*(4), 44–45.

Davidson, H., & Lang, G. (1960). Children's perceptions of their teacher's feelings towards them. *Journal of Experimental Education, 29,* 109–118.

Dinkmeyer, D. (1979). *Systematic training for effective teaching.* Circle Pines, MN: American Guidance Service.

Doyle, W. (1980). *Classroom management.* West Lafayette, IN: Kappa Delta Phi.

Dreikurs, R., Brunwald, B. B., & Pepper, F. C. (1998). *Maintaining sanity in the classroom* (2nd ed.). New York: Harper and Row.

Englander, M. (1989). *Strategies for classroom discipline.* New York: Praeger.

Evertson, C. M., Emmer, E. T., & Worsham, M. E. (1999). *Classroom management for elementary teachers.* Needham Heights, MA: Allyn & Bacon.

Evertson, C. M., & Harris, A. H. (1997). What we know from research about rules and procedures. *COMP [Classroom Organization and Management Program] Workshop Manual.*

Foster, R. M. (1971). Parental communication as a determinant of child behavior. *American Journal of Psychotherapy, 25*(4), 579–590.

Foster, R. M. (1973). A basic strategy for family therapy with children. *American Journal of Psychotherapy, 17*(3), 437–445.

Frieberg, H. J. (1996). From tourists to citizens in the classroom. *Educational Leadership, 54*(1), 32–26.

Ginott, H. G. (1972). *Teacher and child.* New York: MacMillan.

Jenson, W., Sloane, H., & Young, K. R. (1988). *Applied behavior analysis in education: A structured teaching approach.* Englewood Cliffs, NJ: Prentice Hall.

Jones, F. H. (1987). *Positive classroom discipline.* New York: McGraw-Hill.

Kreidler, W. J. (1990). *Elementary perspectives 1: Teaching concepts of peace and conflict.* Cambridge, MA: Educators for Social Responsibility.

Kreidler, W. J. (1994). *Creative resolution in the middle school: A curriculum and teaching guide.* Cambridge, MA: Educators for Social Responsibility.

Lesoff, R. S. (1975). Foster's technique: A systematic approach to family therapy. *Clinical Social Work Journal, 3*(1), 32–45.

Long, N. J., & Newman, R. G. (1980). Managing surface behavior of children in school. In *Conflict in the Classroom: The Education of Emotionally Disturbed Children* (4th ed.). Belmont, CA: Wadsworth.

Lovitt, T. C. (1973). Self-management projects with children with behavior disabilities. *Journal of Learning Disabilities, 6,* 138–150.

McGinnis, E., & Goldstein, A. P. (1990). *Skillstreaming in early childhood: Teaching prosocial skills to the preschool and kindergarten child.* Champaign, IL: Research Press.

McGinnis, E., & Goldstein, A. P. (1997). *Skillstreaming the adolescent: New strategies and perspectives for teaching prosocial skills.* Champaign, IL: Research Press.

McGinnis, E., & Goldstein, A. P. (1997). *Skillstreaming the elementary school child: New strategies and perspectives for teaching prosocial skills.* Champaign, IL: Research Press.

Morgan, D., & Jenson, W. (1988). *Teaching behaviorally disordered students.* Columbus, OH: Merrill Publishing Company.

Morrow, G. (1987). *The compassionate school: A practical guide to educating abused and traumatized children.* Englewood Cliffs, NJ: Prentice Hall.

O'Leary, K. D., & O'Leary, S. G., et al. (1973). *The successful use of behavior modification.* Elmsford, NY: Pergamon Press, Inc.

Paine, S. C. (1983). *Structuring your classroom for academic success.* Champaign, IL: Research Press Company.

Rosenshine, B. (1983). Enthusiastic teaching: A research review. *School Review, 72,* 449–514.

Rosenthal, R. & Jacobson, L. (1968). *Pygmalion in the classroom: Teacher expectation and pupils' intellectual development.* New York: Holt, Rinehart & Winston.

Seeman, H. (2000). *Preventing classroom discipline problems: A guide for educators* (3rd ed.). Laneham, MD: Scarecrow Press.

Smith, M. J. (1975). *When I say no, I feel guilty.* New York: Bantam.

Van Houten, R., et al. (1982). An analysis of some variables influencing the effectiveness of reprimands. *Journal of Applied Behavior Analysis, 15,* 65–83.

Van Houten, R. (1983). *Are social reprimands effective? The effects of punishment on human behavior* (S. Axelrod & J. Apsche, eds.). New York: Academic Press.

Index

Need More Copies or Additional Resources on This Topic?

Solution Tree offers a selection of research-based books, videos, DVDs, and professional development opportunities in the areas of at-risk youth and school improvement.

Schedule professional development time for you and your staff with leading practitioners in the areas of:

Professional Learning Communities
Effective Schools
Assessment *for* **Learning**
Classroom Management
Crisis Management and Response

Order additional related resources by returning the form below or by calling us. Our web site, www.solution-tree.com, also offers online ordering options and much more.

Title	Price*	Quantity	Total
Assertive Discipline, 3rd Edition	$ 19.95		
Assertive Discipline (professional development video kit)	495.00		
Assertive Discipline Plan Book	9.95		
Classroom Management for Academic Success	39.95		
		SUBTOTAL	
SHIPPING			
Continental U.S.: Please add 6% of order total. Outside continental U.S.: Please add 8% of order total.			
		HANDLING	
Continental U.S.: Please add $4. Outside continental U.S.: Please add $6.			
		TOTAL (U.S. funds)	

*Price subject to change without notice.

❏ Check enclosed ❏ Purchase order enclosed

❏ Money order ❏ VISA, MasterCard, Discover, or American Express (circle one)

Credit Card No._____ Exp. Date_____

Cardholder Signature_____

SHIP TO:

First Name_____ Last Name _____

Position_____

Institution Name _____

Address_____

City_____ State_____ ZIP _____

Phone_____ FAX_____

E-mail _____

Solution Tree (formerly National Educational Service)
304 West Kirkwood Avenue
Bloomington, IN 47404
(812) 336-7700 • (800) 733-6786 (toll free) • FAX (812) 336-7790
e-mail: orders@solution-tree.com • www.solution-tree.com

Solution Tree